THE LUCENT LIBRARY OF SCIENCE AND TECHNOLOGY

Bacteria and Viruses

by Peggy Thomas

LUCENT
BOOKS®

THOMSON

™

GALE

San Diego • Detroit • New York • San Francisco • Cleveland • New Haven, Conn. • Waterville, Maine • London • Munich

THOMSON

GALE

On cover: *E.coli* bacteria

© 2004 by Lucent Books ®. Lucent Books ® is an imprint of Thomson Gale, a part of the Thomson Corporation.

Thomson is a trademark and Gale [and Lucent Books] are registered trademarks used herein under license.

For more information, contact
Lucent Books
27500 Drake Rd.
Farmington Hills, MI 48331-3535
Or you can visit our Internet site at http://www.gale.com

LIBRARY OF CONGRESS CATALOGING-IN-PUBLICATION DATA

Thomas, Peggy.
    Bacteria and Viruses / by Peggy Thomas.
        v. cm. — (Lucent library of science and technology)
Includes bibliographical references and index.
Summary: Discusses various types of bacteria and viruses, methods of fighting diseases, and how bacteria and viruses can be used to benefit people and the environment.
    ISBN: 1-59018-438-6

Printed in the United States of America

Table of Contents

Foreword

"The world has changed far more in the past 100 years than in any other century in history. The reason is not political or economic, but technological—technologies that flowed directly from advances in basic science."

— Stephen Hawking, "A Brief History of Relativity," *Time,* 2000

The twentieth-century scientific and technological revolution that British physicist Stephen Hawking describes in the above quote has transformed virtually every aspect of human life at an unprecedented pace. Inventions unimaginable a century ago have not only become commonplace but are now considered necessities of daily life. As science historian James Burke writes, "We live surrounded by objects and systems that we take for granted, but which profoundly affect the way we behave, think, work, play, and in general conduct our lives."

For example, in just one hundred years, transportation systems have dramatically changed. In 1900 the first gasoline-powered motorcar had just been introduced, and only 144 miles of U.S. roads were hard-surfaced. Horse-drawn trolleys still filled the streets of American cities. The airplane had yet to be invented. Today 217 million vehicles speed along 4 million miles of U.S. roads. Humans have flown to the moon and commercial aircraft are capable of transporting passengers across the Atlantic Ocean in less than three hours.

The transformation of communications has been just as dramatic. In 1900 most Americans lived and worked on farms without electricity or mail delivery. Few people had ever heard a radio or spoken on a telephone. A hundred years later, 98 percent of American homes have telephones and televisions and more than 50 percent have personal computers. Some families even have more than one television and computer, and cell phones are now commonplace, even among the young. Data beamed from communication satellites routinely predict global weather conditions and fiber-optic cable, e-mail, and the Internet have made worldwide telecommunication instantaneous.

Perhaps the most striking measure of scientific and technological change can be seen in medicine and public health. At the beginning of the twentieth century, the average American life span was forty-seven years. By the end of the century the average life span was approaching eighty years, thanks to advances in medicine including the development of vaccines and antibiotics, the discovery of powerful diagnostic tools such as X rays, the life-saving technology of cardiac and neonatal care, and improvements in nutrition and the control of infectious disease.

Rapid change is likely to continue throughout the twenty-first century as science reveals more about physical and biological processes such as global warming, viral replication, and electrical conductivity, and as people apply that new knowledge to personal decisions and government policy. Already, for example, an international treaty calls for immediate reductions in industrial and automobile emissions in response to studies that show a potentially dangerous rise in global temperatures is caused by human activity. Taking an active role in determining the direction of future changes depends on education; people must understand the possible uses of scientific research and the effects of the technology that surrounds them.

The Lucent Books Library of Science and Technology profiles key innovations and discoveries that have transformed the modern world. Each title strives to make a complex scientific discovery, technology, or phenomenon understandable and relevant to the reader. Because scientific discovery is rarely straightforward, each title explains the dead ends, fortunate accidents, and basic scientific methods by which the research into the subject proceeded. And every book examines the practical applications of an invention, branch of science, or scientific principle in industry, public health, and personal life, as well as potential future uses and effects based on ongoing research. Fully documented quotations, annotated bibliographies that include both print and electronic sources, glossaries, indexes, and technical illustrations are among the supplemental features designed to point researchers to further exploration of the subject.

Introduction

Swimming in a Sea of Microbes

People do not realize how often they come into contact with bacteria and viruses. These microscopic organisms are in the air, on the surface of this book, and inside people's bodies digesting their last meal. Most people do not fully appreciate that microbes are responsible for the oxygen they breathe, the healthy vegetables on the kitchen table, the pungent cheese in the refrigerator, the clean clothes in the closet, and the clean water coming through the plumbing. Every aspect of people's lives and every part of the natural world is affected, for better or worse, by the actions of bacteria and viruses.

And the worst comes in the form of disease. Even though the overwhelming majority of the encounters with microbes go unnoticed, people are quick to respond when a run-in gives them a runny nose, fever, upset stomach, or more severe symptoms. Some bacteria and viruses cause such pain and devastation that they become headline news. Every year novel microbes are discovered and new infectious diseases emerge. It is not big news when a new bacterium is discovered living harmlessly in the soil, but it is broadcast when a virus mysteriously crops up out of nowhere and kills unsuspecting victims.

The first new disease-causing organism to emerge in the twenty-first century was a virus that appeared in a

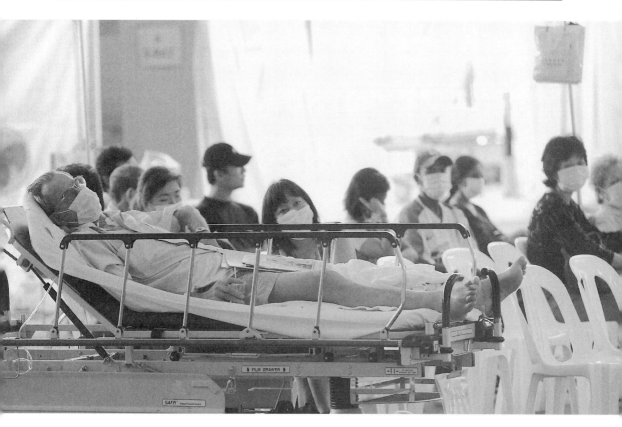

Patients in a Singapore hospital wait to be tested for SARS. The SARS virus was the first new disease-causing organism to be discovered in the twenty-first century.

remote village in China. Researchers may never know how or why the paths of man and microbe crossed, but that fateful event led to the global outbreak in 2003 of SARS (severe acute respiratory syndrome).

Researchers believe the virus's story started inside a wildcat called a civet. Through the natural process of genetic change, the virus gained the ability to infect humans and may have seized the opportunity to do just that when the civet was captured by a hunter or perhaps bought in a marketplace. Whatever the encounter was, it took only days for the first symptoms to appear. At first just a few people came down with a fever and had difficulty breathing. Soon dozens of others in the village grew ill. A doctor treated the patients as best he could, but the mysterious illness would not respond to typical treatments. He had never seen anything like it. It was similar to the flu or pneumonia, but it hit hard and was deadly. Mysteriously the virus avoided children and attacked otherwise healthy adults.

Health officials do know that the doctor traveled to Hong Kong, infecting many of the guests on the ninth floor of a four-star hotel. One of those guests left the hotel and boarded an overseas flight to Toronto, Canada. Along with her luggage, she carried with her the SARS virus. The microorganism proved to be an eager traveler. It unwittingly hitched rides inside its victims to Taiwan, Singapore, Vietnam, and dozens of other countries.

In reaction to this outbreak, the medical community and organizations such as the Centers for Disease Control and the World Health Organization mounted one of the fastest and largest responses in medical history. Even so, in China alone, SARS infected more than five thousand people. It closed schools and businesses and threatened the lives of thousands of people who languished for weeks in quarantine. Outside of China, the virus weakened thousands of people and killed more than eight hundred people worldwide. Economic experts estimated that SARS cost Asian countries more than $30 billion. Toronto, the largest city in Canada, lost $30 million a day because tourists and business travelers were warned to stay away.

When a microbe kills and causes the global panic that SARS did, it is not difficult to imagine it as a malevolent microorganism out to get us. But disease is just the awful side effect of living in a sea of microbes, which are as vital to the planet's web of life as we are. The emergence of a new disease should remind people how interconnected human society is with these invisible organisms. Most of the time people are not aware that they exist. And unlike the clash with the SARS virus, the overwhelming majority of the encounters with microbes are actually good for us.

Chapter 1

We Are Surrounded

We are not alone. No matter how clean we are or how healthy we feel, we carry around on our bodies billions of microbes—microscopic one-celled organisms called bacteria and viruses. Although they cannot be seen, microbes hide under fingernails, lurk between teeth, and live in hair. There are more than six hundred thousand bacteria living on just one square inch of skin, and an average person has about a quarter of a pound of bacteria in and on his or her body at any given time. There are more microbes on a person's body than there are humans on Earth.

Viruses and bacteria are responsible for some of the deadliest diseases in history, such as AIDS, the plague, and flu. And yet bacteria perform the most important roles in maintaining life on this planet. "They [bacteria] protect us and feed us," says Abigail Salyers, former president of the American Society for Microbiology. "All life on Earth depends on their activities."[1] Bacteria are the planet's recyclers, plant nurturers, and undertakers.

Microbes have been found in almost every type of environment. Some thrive in subzero Arctic ice, while others live in boiling undersea volcanoes. Bacteria have been found inside oil-drilling cores pulled from more than a thousand feet down in the earth's crust, and it has been estimated that there may be as much as 100 trillion tons of bacteria deep beneath the surface of the earth. If all the subterranean microbes were brought to the surface, they would cover the planet with a layer five feet deep. Microbes have been discovered six miles beneath the Pacific Ocean, where the pressure is equivalent to being squashed by fifty jumbo jets, as well as nineteen miles out in space.

Professor Adrian Gibbs of the Australian National University asserts, "You can increase the probability of finding new things by looking in interesting places, like deep sea vents or thermal pools, but you can also find them in your own backyard."[2] One teaspoon of ordinary soil contains 10 million bacteria, and one acre of soil can hold up to five hundred pounds of microscopic life. There is more unseen life than seen. The mass of all microbes on the planet is twenty-five times more than the mass of all other animals combined. The human race may believe it is at the top of the food chain, but microbes are the food chain.

Microbes can thrive in almost any environment, from subzero Arctic ice to boiling underwater volcanoes.

Ancient Microbes

How did these organisms become so widespread? The answer lies in the fossil record. Scientist J. William Schopf found evidence of ancient microbes in rock samples collected in western Australia in the 1980s. These rocks proved that bacteria had been on Earth for more than 3.5 billion years, long enough to adapt to nearly every type of environment. In his book *Cradle of Life,* Schopf notes, "These organisms are not only extremely ancient but surprisingly advanced, and show that early evolution proceeded faster and faster than anyone imagined."[3] Scientists have even discovered a strain of bacteria that can survive blasts of radiation one thousand times greater than the amount needed to kill a human being.

Bacteria and viruses have infected humans for thousands of years. Some Egyptian mummies bear scars or other evidence of viral disease.

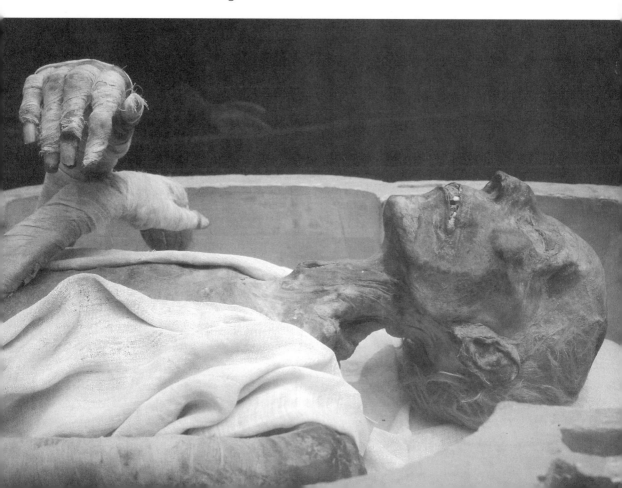

Scientists have not found fossil evidence of ancient viruses and may never do so because viruses are so small. But researchers believe that viruses have been around just as long as bacteria have, or even longer. Deadly viruses may have played a part in the extinction of the dinosaurs and are thought to have contributed to human evolution.

Historians do know that bacteria and viruses infected human civilizations as far back as three thousand years ago. The mummy of Egyptian pharaoh Ramses V has the telltale signs of scars caused by the deadly smallpox virus. The shriveled arms and legs of other mummies suggest that these people suffered from the polio virus. And the Bible describes an ancient plague, reminiscent of anthrax, which caused "sores that break into pustules on man and beast."[4]

Bacteria

One reason scientists believe that microbes have survived for so long is their simple structure. A bacterium is a primitive one-celled organism. Like all living things, it grows, uses energy, makes waste, and reproduces all within one cell. A hard cell wall made of cellulose provides support and protects the bacteria from antibiotic substances, such as medicines, tears, and saliva. An inner lining, called the cell membrane, acts as the gatekeeper controlling what goes in and out. Some bacteria also have a sticky outer coat, called a capsule, that allows the bacteria to stick to other cells.

Bacteria come in three basic shapes: Cocci (pronounced cox-eye) are shaped like little round balls; bacilli (buh-sill-eye) are rod- or stick-shaped; and spirilla (spy-rill-uh) form a spiral. Scientists estimate that there may be a million species of bacteria in the world and more than five thousand different viruses, but only a small fraction of these has ever been studied.

Some bacteria exist as individual cells floating on their own, while others cluster together to form pairs that scientists call diplo. Several bacteria strung together in a chain are called strepto, and when bacteria stick together in clusters, they are referred to as staphylo.

Bacteria have a wide-ranging diet. Some bacteria are capable of photosynthesis, just like plants. They make their own food from sunlight and give off oxygen. These bacteria are called cyanobacteria. Although these aquatic organisms are often referred to as blue-green algae, that name is misleading because they are not related to other types of algae.

Other bacteria absorb nutrients from the materials that surround them. There are bacteria that feed off of wood, glue, paint, and anything dripped, dribbled, or left out on the kitchen counter too long. Others eat iron, sulfur, petroleum, a variety of toxic chemicals, and even radioactive plutonium. The bacteria that live in a person's stomach absorb the nutrients from ingested food. A rotten spot on an apple is evidence that bacteria are eating. The sour smell of old milk is a clue that bacteria are there. And the feeling of fuzzy teeth in the morning is evidence that bacteria are at work.

Although most bacteria cannot move about their environment on their own, some have flagella, long whiplike tails that propel bacteria through a drop of liquid. One bacterium's flagellum was recorded moving twenty-four hundred beats per minute. Other bacteria are not as speedy. They secrete a slime that allows them to slide over surfaces like a slug, or they move with the help of cilia, tiny hairlike structures that beat wildly.

Bacteria move in response to their environment. While studying *Escherichia coli* (the bacteria that live in human intestines and can sometimes cause diarrhea), researchers identified special structures called nose spots. These nose spots allow the bacterium to sense the presence of food and move toward it. They also detect toxins and move away from them. These nose spots are extremely sensitive and can perceive tiny changes in the surrounding environment. It is the same degree of sensitivity that would allow a person to detect the difference between a jar with 9,999 pennies and one with 10,000 pennies. When food is detected, the receptors send a message to the flagella, which then beat rhythmically, carrying the bacteria toward the increased concentration of food.

When food is not available, bacteria are capable of lying dormant for many years in the form of a spore. Spores of anthrax have been found in eighty-year-old museum displays; other bacterial spores have been brought back

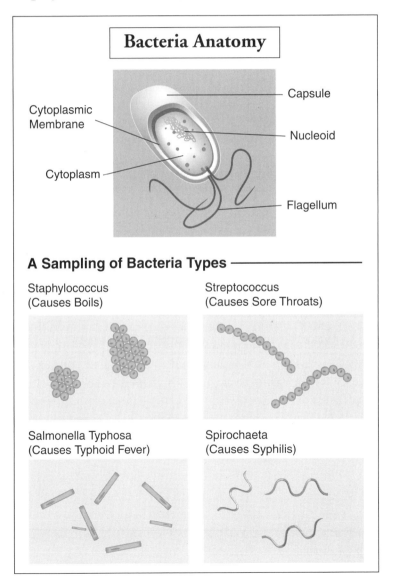

Bacteria Anatomy

Capsule

Cytoplasmic Membrane

Nucleoid

Cytoplasm

Flagellum

A Sampling of Bacteria Types

Staphylococcus
(Causes Boils)

Streptococcus
(Causes Sore Throats)

Salmonella Typhosa
(Causes Typhoid Fever)

Spirochaeta
(Causes Syphilis)

to an active state from cans of meat that were 118 years old and beer that was 166 years old. Russian scientists even claim to have brought back to life bacteria that was frozen in Arctic ice for a million years.

Spores are hard to find because they are microscopic. All bacteria are measured in nanometers. One nanometer is one-billionth of a meter. The period at the end of this sentence is about 1 million nanometers in diameter. The average bacterium, in comparison, is only one thousand nanometers across.

Bacteria are small, but viruses are even smaller. To get an idea of their size, imagine one human cell the size of a baseball diamond. In that cell, an average bacterium would be the size of the pitcher's mound. But a single virus would be the size of a baseball. Scientists need to use a powerful piece of equipment called an electron microscope to enter the world of the virus.

Viruses

Bacteria and viruses are often grouped together under the heading of microbes, but there are vast differences between them, and size is just one of those differences. While bacteria perform all of the functions necessary to be considered a life form, scientists debate whether viruses are alive at all. For something to be alive it must eat, grow, make waste, and reproduce. When a virus is floating around in the air or sitting undisturbed in soil, it is no more alive than a rock. But if that same virus comes in contact with a suitable animal, plant, or bacterium cell, it suddenly becomes active. A virus does not eat, but it gets its energy from the host cell it infects. It does not grow in the sense that it gets larger, but it does reproduce. In fact, a virus's sole purpose seems to be reproduction, and it cannot do that without the help of a living cell.

A virus is not even considered a true cell. It is simply a tiny bundle of genetic material, DNA (deoxyribonucleic acid) or RNA (ribonucleic acid), surrounded by a protein coat. Both DNA and RNA are the molecules that contain coded genetic information. They

A Sampling of Viruses

Human
Immunodeficiency
Virus (HIV)

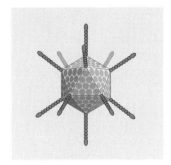

Adenovirus
(Causes respiratory infections
and intestinal tract infections.)

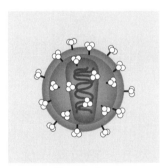

Coronavirus
(Causes SARS, colds,
and pneumonia.)

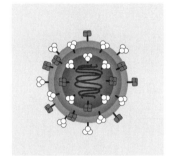

Influenza Virus

make up genes that determine what an organism looks like and how it behaves. Unlike the DNA in an animal or plant cell that is contained in a nucleus, viral DNA floats loosely within the protein coat, or capsid.

Like bacteria, viruses come in many shapes and sizes. Many are multisided and look like a cut diamond. Other viruses are shaped like sticks, ovals with spikes, or tiny sausages. The deadly Ebola virus looks like a piece of looped string. Viruses that attack bacteria are called bacteriophages and resemble tiny lunar landing modules or alien spaceships.

Microbial Multiplication

Microbes are experts at mass production. Bacteria reproduce through a process called binary fission. One cell divides into two cells, each of which then divide into two more. Each cell is identical to the mother cell. Most bacteria divide every two or three hours, some wait as long as sixteen hours, and others are capable

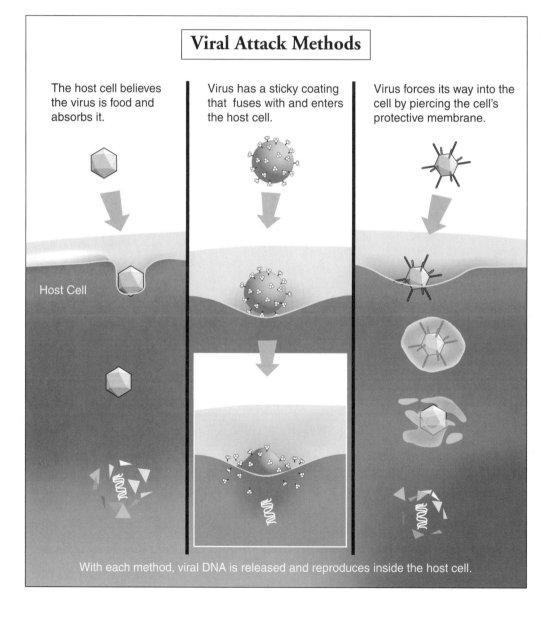

Viral Attack Methods

The host cell believes the virus is food and absorbs it.

Virus has a sticky coating that fuses with and enters the host cell.

Virus forces its way into the cell by piercing the cell's protective membrane.

Host Cell

With each method, viral DNA is released and reproduces inside the host cell.

of dividing every fifteen minutes. One researcher estimated that if one bacterium reproduced every twenty minutes without running out of food or encountering any toxins, it would grow into a colony of 2 million bacteria within seven hours.

Viruses are just as productive, but they cannot do it alone. Viruses need the reproductive mechanisms of a living cell in order to multiply, but first the virus must get inside the cell. A cell's membrane is made out of protein molecules, and some molecules have specially shaped receptors, or landing sites, where other molecules with matching shapes can land and dock. This lock-and-key system allows the entry of only certain molecules that are necessary for normal cell function. For example, essential nutrients such as oxygen are allowed to pass through the membrane to one of many of the cell's powerhouses, the mitochondria. Nitrogen is received at different sites on the membrane and shuttled through to be used in the assembly of various proteins.

But viruses have also acquired the key to specific cells. For example, the pneumonia virus is capable of latching on to a human lung cell. The virus that causes hepatitis can infect human liver cells. The human immunodeficiency virus (HIV) that causes AIDS is capable of landing on white blood cells.

Once a virus attaches to a host cell, it inserts its genetic material in one of three ways. Some host cells are fooled into thinking that the virus is food. These cells pull the genetic material in just as they would pull in other nutrients. Other viruses have a sticky coat that fuses with the cell's membrane, and the genetic material enters that way. Other viruses forcibly pierce the cell's membrane and inject their DNA into the host.

The genetic material from the virus hijacks the reproductive machinery of the host cell and provides it with a new set of instructions to follow. The cell is now programmed to make hundreds of copies of the virus's DNA or RNA instead of its own.

The virus then uses the cell's enzymes, which are molecules that control chemical changes, to build new capsids and other proteins it needs to survive. Like a genetic factory, the host cell churns out viral parts that are assembled into brand-new identical viruses. All other cell functions are shut down to conserve energy for producing as many viruses as the cell can stand. Some cells simply fall apart from exhaustion, and viruses tumble free. But other viruses actively dissolve the cell membrane to get out. Stronger cells will fill up with viruses until they burst like an overfilled water balloon. The new viruses are free to infect other host cells, a process that spreads the disease. This continues until the virus is stopped or the host dies.

Microbes at Work

Other microbes can cause the death of their hosts too, but the vast majority of bacteria play a vital role in Earth's ecosystem. All life on Earth is connected in a web of relationships. Every creature, no matter how small, has a job to do, and microbes are the workhorses of the living world.

Bacteria keep the planet's life cycles turning. It is an important job because the earth is a closed system. There is only a limited amount of the materials that sustain all living things, and these elements—oxygen, carbon, hydrogen, nitrogen, phosphorus, and so on— have to be recycled again and again. Microbes are the key players, chemists building, breaking down, and re-building chemical compounds for both animal and plant use. For example, animals breathe in oxygen and exhale carbon dioxide (CO_2). Plants take in that CO_2 and release oxygen that will be taken up again by animals. Microbes beneath the sea pump out about 150 billion kilograms of oxygen every year, producing one-half of all the oxygen we breathe. This recycling process seems simplistic on the surface, but scientists are awed by the complexity of this assembly-line efficiency that is required to keep the earth's ecosystem cycling. If that system were to stop, all the oxygen in the air would be exhausted within twenty years.

A similarly complex cycle occurs for nitrogen. Nitrogen exists in every living cell and is necessary for building proteins. Although nitrogen is the most common gas in the atmosphere, animals cannot use it in that form. Animals get their nitrogen from eating plants or eating plant eaters. Most plants are also unable to take nitrogen from the air; they get their cell-building nitrogen from the soil. But most plants cannot get the nitrogen they need without the help of nitrogen-fixing bacteria. These bacteria "fix" the nitrogen by combining the nitrogen in the atmosphere with other elements to form organic compounds in living cells. When these cells later die, the nitrogen, now in a fixed form, is readily available to the plants through their root systems with the help of other bacteria in the soil. In return, the plant supplies the microbes with nutrients for their growth. Some bacteria simply live in the soil surrounding the roots, but other kinds of bacteria actually live inside the roots of plants.

Farmers rejuvenate their fields by planting nitrogen-fixing crops such as the pea plant. These plants have a powerful partnership with a bacterium called *Rhizobium*. As a young pea plant sends out its roots, it also sends out a signal to willing bacteria. The bacteria in the soil migrate to the roots, where they are surrounded by and eventually become part of the roots. An uprooted pea or clover plant reveals tiny nodules or bumps where the bacteria are working to fix nitrogen for the plant. In return, the plant provides the bacteria with a safe home and the nutrients they need to live. This system is very effective. Researchers estimate that the bacteria living in Asian rice paddies are capable of fixing more than six hundred pounds of nitrogen per acre.

Decomposition
Another job of the microbial chemists is to free up the essential chemical compounds that are trapped in

plants and animals and would otherwise remain trapped after death. Bacteria (along with fungi) are the undertakers of the microbial world. Bacteria help break down the dead matter in a process called decomposition. If all the microbes were wiped out suddenly, nothing would rot. We would eventually be knee-deep in dead organisms.

All living things only borrow their atoms. They must be continually rotated and returned to the soil so that other plants and animals can grow. The fertilizers that people put on their lawns are nothing more than mixtures of chemical compounds of phosphorus, nitrogen, sulfur, and potassium, the same elements that are released into the soil by the decomposing activities of microbes.

The Bacterial Buddy System

Just as some bacteria form partnerships with plants, other bacteria form partnerships with animals. One of the most common relationships involves bacteria digesting other animals' food.

Ruminant animals like cattle, sheep, goats, giraffes, and camels are incapable of digesting cellulose, a tough, protective structural substance that forms plant cell walls. Yet leafy greens are their prime food source. The only creatures known to digest cellulose are microbes, so the only way ruminant animals can get any nutrition from plants is to harbor a healthy amount of bacteria in two of their four stomachs. The first two stomachs in the digestive system of a cow contain billions of bacteria that break down the cellulose into glucose, which the cow's cells can use.

Humans rely on bacteria to digest the cellulose in food too. When babies are born, their mouths and digestive tracts are sterile; there are no microbes living there yet. Newborns have been protected from all infection, including beneficial microbes, by the placenta. But the first time babies are fed, they get the bacteria they need to digest food for the rest of their lives.

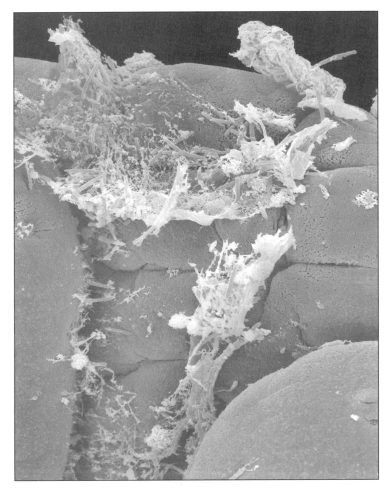

An electron micrograph shows bacteria at work breaking down food in the human digestive tract.

Besides breaking down tough cellulose in a person's diet, the bacteria that live in the large intestine also produce essential vitamins (K, B_{12}, thiamine, and riboflavin) that humans could not make themselves. Studies of animals born and raised in a sterile environment show how vital microbes are to survival. Without them a person would have a whole host of problems. Without vitamin K, which is necessary in the clotting process of blood, a person would be prone to uncontrolled bleeding. Without vitamin B_{12}, a person would suffer from a blood disorder called pernicious anemia. Scientists did not realize the importance of bacteria in our digestive system until the development of antibiotics. They were surprised to find that people developed digestive problems when taking an antibiotic. The drug killed the "good" bacteria in the intestines as well as the "bad" bacteria that made them sick.

Viruses and Evolution

Microbiologists are discovering new information every day about the important roles bacteria play in the world's ecosystem. But no one has yet discovered if viruses have a beneficial function. Recent studies suggest that viruses may play some part in the adaptations that change species over time. Geneticists have found bits and pieces of viral DNA inside animal cells. These small fragments were probably left behind from a time when that animal was infected with the virus. While the host cells were reproducing the virus's DNA parts, the genetic material was pulled into the host's genes. There they survived in the host's cells and were passed down to the animal's offspring.

Geneticists discovered that this "junk" DNA accounts for nearly half of a person's genetic material, or genome. "People started to seriously consider that they [viruses] might contribute to evolution,"[5] says John McDonald, a molecular evolutionist at the University of Georgia. Certain viral genes may have caused significant changes in human looks and behavior or even the branching off of man from ape 6 million years ago.

Bacteria and viruses have inhabited the earth much longer than humans have and were performing important tasks long before we arrived. Microbiologists are still learning the intricate connections that link the microbe's existence with our own. The smallest organisms on Earth have had a powerful effect. They have even altered the course of human history.

Chapter 2

Early Discoveries

It is impossible for the human tongue to recount the awful truth. . . . The victims died almost immediately. They would swell beneath the armpits and in the groin and fall over while talking. Father abandoned child, wife husband, one brother another; for this illness seemed to strike through breath and sight. . . . In many places . . . great pits were dug and piled deep with the multitude of dead. And they died by the hundreds, both day and night.[6]

Agnolo di Tura chronicled this tragic yet common occurrence in Siena, Italy, in 1348. Called the Great Pestilence, the disease was later known as the Black Death or bubonic plague, and it swept through Europe with frightening speed. Spread by the bite of an infected flea, the *Yersinia pestis* bacteria caused the most devastation recorded in human history. Within four years it killed one-third of the population of Europe, more than 25 million people.

The first symptom to strike a plague victim was a severe headache. The victim would grow weaker and eventually too tired to walk. After about three days the lymph nodes in the victim's armpits and groin swelled to the size of goose eggs. These swellings, called buboes, gave the disease its name—the bubonic plague. The victim's heart would futilely try to pump blood throughout the swollen areas. Blood vessels broke, causing widespread hemorrhaging that blackened the skin. Soon the patient would cough up blood and the nervous system would collapse, causing their limbs to jerk in fits of pain.

Once the lungs became infected, the disease could be transmittable from person to person through the air. At that stage, it was called pneumonic plague, and it swept through villages like wildfire. Within a week the patient was dead.

"I, Agnolo di Tura, buried my five children with my own hands. . . . And so many died that all believed it was the end of the world."[7]

The world did not end, but it did change drastically. With more than a third of the population gone, laborers were in high demand. Large tracts of land were suddenly available for those once too poor to own

A nineteenth-century painting depicts the agony of plague victims. The Black Death of the 1340s, the worst outbreak of plague in history, decimated Europe's population.

property. The wealthy became wealthier still, as they accumulated the riches of their dead relatives. Those who survived the epidemic experienced a time of rejuvenation.

They also experienced a time of doubt and inquiry. The methods for dealing with the plague had failed miserably. Many physicians began questioning the validity of the ancient Roman medical philosophies that had been the foundation of all their knowledge. Some began to study the human anatomy and develop new methods of treating the sick. Rather than relying on traditional methods, scientists began proposing new theories of disease and experimenting to prove or disprove their theories. An invisible bacterium capable of killing millions changed history and opened the door to an era known for its startling new ideas—the Renaissance.

Smallpox and the New World

Microbes had an impact on history in the Americas as well. The Caribbean island of Hispaniola had more than a million inhabitants when Christopher Columbus landed there in 1492. Within twenty years, more than a third of the population was dead. Some died at the hands of cruel Spanish masters, others starved to death, but the majority of native islanders died from an epidemic disease they had never seen before—smallpox.

Breathing in the invisible virus particles from an infected person's sneeze or cough spread the smallpox virus from person to person. A week after inhaling these particles, an infected person came down with a high fever, body aches, a headache, and chills. Soon the victim broke out in a flame-red rash that grew fiery, raised, and blistered. These sores or pustules gave the virus its name, variola, derived from the Latin word for spotted. A person who survived might have scars or be permanently blinded. More severe cases that attacked the internal organs resulted in death. This devastating disease spread quickly through a population that had no resistance.

The same thing happened when Hernán Cortés invaded the Aztec city of Tenochtitlán, where he and his soldiers were soundly defeated by the Aztec army. But as the Spaniards fled, they unwittingly left behind a time bomb in the form of a dead Spanish soldier infected with smallpox. Within weeks, the entire capital was under siege by the smallpox virus, which killed one-fourth of the city's inhabitants. According to one Spanish priest, "In many places it happened that everyone in a house died and, as it was impossible to bury the great number of dead, they pulled down the houses over them so that their homes became their tombs."[8]

The smallpox epidemic spread throughout Mexico and helped the Spaniards defeat the Inca Empire as well. Without the help of the deadly smallpox virus and other epidemics, the Europeans might not have so easily conquered the New World. Smallpox also traveled to Brazil with the Portuguese, killing tens of thousands of Indians there, and marched north to North America with the British, French, and Danish explorers, wiping out scores of Native American villages and entire tribes. The terror was universal. According to one French missionary stationed in Canada, "The contagion increased as autumn advanced; and when winter came . . . its ravages were appalling. The season of Huron festivity was turned to a season of mourning."[9]

Other infectious diseases caused by bacteria and viruses may not have had such a profound effect on the world order as the bubonic plague and smallpox, but they also weakened armies, wiped out villages, attacked the poor, and cast blame on those who were different.

Punishment from the Gods

Where could these horrific diseases come from? They mysteriously came upon a person, gripping him or her with terrible symptoms and then quickly spread through a community. Ethnic and religious groups were often blamed for the disease.

Prior to the 1800s most people believed that epidemics like the plague and smallpox were punishments from God. Describing the plague that hit Italy in 1347, the Italian writer Giovanni Boccaccio suggested that the plague signified God's anger at people's wicked way of life. And when the Black Death ravaged England three years later, the archbishop of York said, "This surely must be caused by the sins of men." [10]

In India, people worshipped Sitala, the goddess of smallpox. Known as the "cool one," she had the power to relieve raging fevers. In paintings and sculptures Sitala is portrayed dressed in red, riding a donkey. She carries a cup of water to cool a victim's wilting thirst and a broom to sweep away the disease. Although people bestowed

English nurses tend to smallpox patients in this nineteenth-century illustration. Although a vaccine exists today, deadly outbreaks of smallpox have been common throughout history.

her with offerings of cool drinks and chilled food, they also feared her, for Sitala could inflict the disease on the undeserving as well. It seemed only reasonable to blame the mysterious illness on a higher power. After all, no one could see another cause.

The earliest written record suggesting that invisible living things might cause illness came from the Roman writer Marcus Terentius Varro. In the first century A.D. he wrote, "Care should be taken where there are swamps in the neighborhood, because certain tiny creatures which cannot be seen by the eyes breed there. These float through the air and enter the body by the mouth and nose and cause serious disease."[11]

Microbes Come into View

Perhaps Varro was not the only one who suspected that a living organism invisible to the naked eye could exist, let alone cause the deadly destruction that plagued humankind. But it was not a popular thought. There was no evidence that these tiny creatures inhabited the world until a curious amateur scientist named Antoni van Leeuwenhoek saw them for the first time in 1676.

By profession, Leeuwenhoek was a draper (a cloth dealer) who examined threads for flaws with a magnifying glass. His fascination with magnifying lenses and the world they brought into view led him to experiment with single-lens microscopes he made himself. While others used microscopes that enlarged objects only ten times their size, Leeuwenhoek's microscope could magnify up to 270 times. His lenses were so finely made that experts today still are not sure how they were constructed given the technology of the seventeenth century.

What Leeuwenhoek saw under his microscope would open up a new field of science called microbiology. After looking at the matter he picked from between his teeth, Leeuwenhoek recorded for the first time the presence of what are now known as bacteria. He described them as "animacules, very prettily a-moving. The biggest sort had a very strong and swift motion, and shot through the water like a pike does through the water; mostly these were of small numbers." [12]

In the seventeenth century, Antoni van Leeuwenhoek invented this powerful single-lens microscope.

Although Leeuwenhoek was the first person to describe bacteria, the scientific community did not take his observations seriously. In 1676 the secretary of the Royal Society in London, wrote to Leeuwenhoek: "Your letter . . . has been received here with amusement. Your account of myriad 'little animals' seen swimming in rainwater, with the aid of your so-called 'microscope,' caused the members of the society considerable merriment when read at our most recent meeting." [13] The members of the Royal Society declined to publish Leeuwenhoek's observations until 1683, when they received more evidence. In the meantime, Leeuwenhoek continued to study pond water, spittle from an old man, insect larvae, and even the spermatozoa in semen. Leeuwenhoek brought the world beneath the microscope into view, but it would take one hundred years before these invisible creatures would be linked with disease.

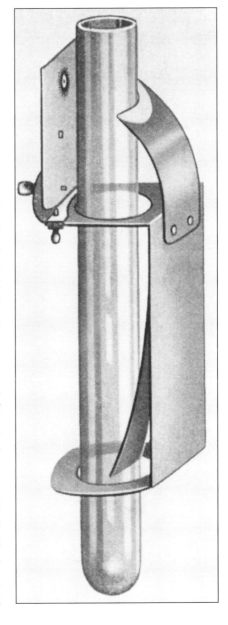

Putting It All Together

Throughout the 1860s, two scientists, Louis Pasteur of France and Robert Koch of Germany, working independently, collected convincing evidence that infectious diseases were caused by microbes and not by evil spirits or the wrath of God.

Pasteur was a chemist and microbiologist working in France. In his studies of wine making for the wine industry, he learned that microscopic bacteria and yeast organisms caused fermentation, the chemical breakdown of carbohydrates into carbon dioxide and alcohol. He went on to identify the microorganisms that caused food to spoil and decompose. Before his discovery, people assumed that spoilage was the natural result of chemical breakdown over time. Pasteur found the microbes in milk that caused it to spoil and also devised pasteurization—the process of heating milk to a certain temperature at which harmful bacteria are killed.

After Pasteur's success in the wine industry, the silk manufacturers of France consulted him about the mysterious deaths of their prized silkworms. Pasteur identified two different bacteria that caused the deadly silkworm disease. Pasteur's work provided the world with

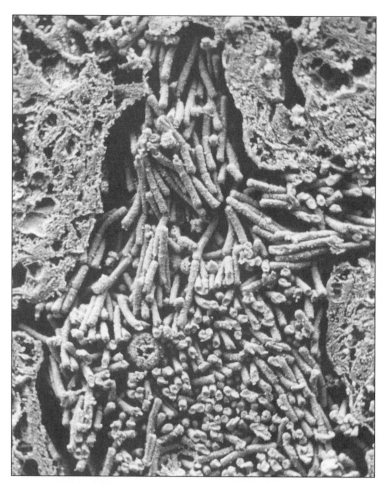

Anthrax bacteria infect lung tissue. In a series of laboratory experiments with mice, Robert Koch was able to isolate the deadly anthrax bacterium.

convincing evidence that microorganisms cause disease, a concept that became known as the germ theory. Around the same time in Germany, medical doctor and researcher Robert Koch was also putting some of the pieces of the bacterial puzzle together.

Robert Koch

Koch was experimenting with ways to grow bacteria in the lab when he developed the process for growing bacteria that is still followed today. By using a gelatin-like substance called agar, which is made from seaweed, rather than blood or tissue from an animal, pure bacterial cultures could be grown without contamination from other blood or tissue cells. Koch's assistant, Julius Petri, created a covered shallow glass dish to hold the agar and the growing culture. Today this commonly used piece of lab equipment bears his name—a petri dish.

Another problem Koch struggled with was making bacteria more visible under a microscope. Some bacteria are very difficult to see, especially if they are mixed with other cells. Through experimentation Koch found that bacteria absorbed a dye made from coal tar, called aniline dye, which made them easier to see under the microscope.

At the time Koch was perfecting his lab techniques, anthrax was a common and debilitating disease that attacked cattle and sheep throughout Europe. Parts of Germany were hard hit by the disease, and Koch set out to isolate the bacterium that caused it. He injected mice with blood taken from the spleens of infected animals and observed how the disease worked as he transferred it from one mouse to another. His study of disease led him to write the criteria that are still used to determine if a microorganism is the cause of a disease. Called Koch's postulates, these criteria state that a pathogenic (disease-causing) organism must be present in every case of the disease. This organism can then be grown, or "cultured," outside the body. An animal inoculated with the culture would develop the same disease. The organism could then be taken from that infected animal and cultured again.

Koch went on to isolate the bacteria that caused tuberculosis and chicken cholera, and Pasteur used Koch's lab methods to expand on his work with anthrax. In order to create a vaccine for sheep, Pasteur weakened the anthrax bacterium by growing it in the lab at higher temperatures than normal. When this weakened bacteria was injected into a healthy animal, it prevented infection from the virulent anthrax bacteria and became an effective vaccine. Pasteur went on to create a vaccine for chicken cholera and rabies.

By the end of the nineteenth century the germ theory was accepted as a scientific principle. Only one problem remained. For some diseases, no microorganisms could be found.

What Could Be Smaller than Bacteria?

Although Pasteur created a vaccine for rabies, he never saw the organism that caused this dreaded disease. Many other scientists who worked on plant and animal infections assumed they were looking for bacteria, but they would never find them. What they did find was something smaller and more puzzling.

In 1886 Adolf Mayer, a German scientist, was researching the tobacco mosaic disease, so called because it left the leaves of the tobacco plant shriveled and mottled. Mayer believed that the disease was caused by a bacterium, but he failed to isolate the elusive organism. In 1892 Russian scientist Dmitri Ivanovski ruled out the possibility that a bacterium caused all the damage to the tobacco plant. He suggested that a smaller pathogen must be at work, possibly a toxin. It was not until six years later that Martinus Beijerinck, a scientist from the Netherlands, showed that the disease was indeed caused by an infectious agent smaller than any other life-form known.

Ivanovski and Beijerinck performed similar experiments. They pressed juice from infected plants through filters so fine that they removed all bacteria. When this filtered liquid was rubbed onto a healthy plant, it caused the leaves to shrivel and discolor. Both scientists discovered that the plant juice could be diluted many, many times and still cause disease. And although they suspected a bacteria-like organism might be at work, it could not be grown separately in a petri dish.

Where Ivanovski and Beijerinck differed was in their conclusions. Beijerinck believed that whatever passed through his filters was some kind of an infective agent

Dutch botanist Martinus Beijerinck was the first scientist to identify viruses, infectious microbes that are even smaller than bacteria.

other than bacteria. He did not believe it was simply a toxin, as Ivanovski suggested. Beijerinck filtered and diluted the infective liquid again and again until he was left with such a weak substance that if it were a toxin, it would no longer harm the plant. But when this diluted substance was rubbed onto a healthy tobacco leaf, it shriveled and the disease spread to other parts of the plant. Attempts to grow the organism in the lab failed. Whatever it was, the infective agent would grow and spread only inside plant cells.

In 1898 Beijerinck wrote his conclusions. Using the Latin term for poison, he called the elusive particle a filterable virus. He showed that although it could not be seen, the virus was an infective agent that was not conducive to being cultured in a lab. In his paper he observed, "The contagion, to reproduce itself must be incorporated into the living cytoplasm of the cell into whose multiplication it is, as it were, passively drawn."[14]

Building on Beijerinck's virus theory, new discoveries were made in rapid succession. That same year, Friedrich Loeffler and Paul Frosch discovered the virus that caused foot-and-mouth disease, which had been killing cattle throughout Europe. They collected pus from the sores of infected cattle and passed it through a filter. They did not find a bacterium, but they did discover that when the so-called filterable virus was injected into a healthy animal, it caused the disease.

It was not until 1900 that a filterable virus was discovered to cause human disease. Yellow fever had been rampant and troublesome throughout Central and South America. It caused almost insurmountable problems for the builders of the Panama Canal. Cuban doctor Carlos Juan Finlay suspected that a mosquito, *Aedes aegypti,* spread the disease. But this idea did not receive much attention until U.S. Army doctor Major Walter Reed traveled to Cuba and conducted medical experiments. He discovered that the disease was caused by a filterable virus and confirmed that a mosquito was in-

Viral Replication

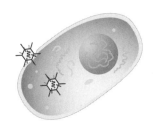

The virus particle first attaches to and then injects itself into the host cell.

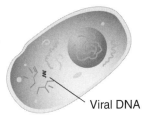

The viral wall breaks down and the DNA contained inside is released.

Viral DNA

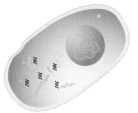

The viral DNA replicates itself; the new copies are made from raw materials within the host cell.

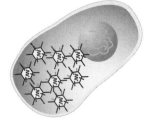

Each of the new copies of the viral DNA now directs the manufacture of a wall for itself.

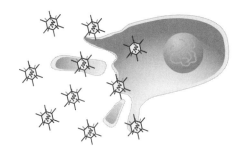

The newly formed viral particles are released in large numbers, and the host cell may be destroyed.

deed the vector (it carried the virus from person to person).

Fifteen years later brought the discovery of a virus that infected bacteria. It was called a bacteriophage (bacteria eater). The definition of a virus was taking shape—an organism that could be passed through the finest filter and still cause an infectious disease in plants, animals, humans, or bacteria. The organism, however, could not be seen and could not be grown in a laboratory. It was not until the 1930s that scientists got their first glimpse of their smallest enemy.

Viruses Come into View

Improvements in microscope manufacturing did not help the search for viruses until a revolutionary machine was invented. In the 1930s German researchers Max Knott and Ernst Ruska created the electron microscope.

Instead of using an ordinary beam of light to illuminate an object, the electron microscope uses electrons, which are accelerated in a vacuum until their wavelength is extremely short. The beams of these fast-moving electrons are then focused on cells. The electrons are absorbed or scattered by the cell's parts and form an image on an electrosensitive photographic plate. This technique allows the microscope to magnify an image up to 1 million times.

For the first time scientists could see the shape of viruses. But the electron microscope still did not reveal what a virus was made of or how it was constructed. That breakthrough came in 1932, when chemist Wendell Stanley used a technique called X-ray crystallography to transform the tobacco mosaic virus into a crystal. This was an amazing feat. Because crystallization is a characteristic of a mineral, a nonliving thing, Stanley's achievement proved that a virus is not a typical living organism. It is essentially a chemical molecule, a protein, with minute bits of genetic material. This discovery won Stanley the Nobel Prize in Chemistry.

The bulk of what was discovered about microbes in the early years of microbiology was through the study of disease and disease-causing bacteria and viruses. One prime goal was finding a way to destroy them.

Chapter 3

Fighting an Invisible Enemy

Humans have evolved along with bacteria and viruses for millions of years, so it should be no surprise that the human body has developed a system of keeping the harmful microbes out. The first line of defense is the skin, which is a sheath of closely interlocking cells. Sweat and oil glands under the skin secrete acids that prevent the growth of microbes, and harmless bacteria that normally live on the body defend their territories against foreign bacteria.

The nose, mouth, and throat are common sites of attack, but fragile membranes and layers of sticky mucus that are toxic to harmful microbes protect them. Tears and saliva also contain antiseptic substances. Bacteria and viruses are sneezed out, coughed up, and cried out of the body. If microbes make it through these barriers, they are swallowed. Most will not survive in the stomach's acid environment or the toxic world of the intestines. The beneficial bacteria that reside there will fight off potential competitors.

Our Internal Army

A cut on the skin is a way in for some opportunistic microbes, but the body quickly fights back with an inflammatory response. Injured cells release histamine, a chemical that causes blood vessels near a wound to swell, which brings more blood to the area to aid healing.

Blood quickly clots to seal off the cut and prevent more bacteria from getting into the bloodstream and spreading further into the body.

Injured cells also release a chemical that attracts bacteria-eating white cells called phagocytes. Phagocytes engulf any bacteria they encounter until they are so full they die. Any bacteria that manage to get past the phagocytes will be carried to other parts of the body. The body's immune system is alerted and sends out lymphocytes, or white cells. There are about 2 trillion lymphocytes patrolling a person's bloodstream and lymph system at any given time. They stand guard in the spleen, tonsils, and lymph nodes and detect all foreign invaders such as bacteria, viruses, fungi, and transplanted organs.

When a foreign invader is detected, the lymphocytes divide and create antibodies to kill or neutralize the invaders. Antibodies are chemicals that target and destroy only one type of invader. For example, an antibody sent out to fight against the pneumonia bacterium cannot fight a salmonella bacterium. It takes about a week to generate enough antibodies to fight a disease. In that time, it is a race for survival between man and microbe.

The immune system has an ingenious way of remembering past battles so that this life-and-death struggle does not happen again. Lymphocytes create memory cells that circulate through the body ready to battle the old enemy. If a person comes down with the same strain of pneumonia a second time, the memory cells kick into maximum production immediately. Some memory cells last a lifetime, which provides immunity against that disease for the rest of a person's life. That is why a person who has had chicken pox will not get it again. This amazing immune response is the principle behind vaccinations.

Ancient Asian Secrets

Smallpox ravaged Asia for generations, yet as early as the eleventh century there was a method of fighting

The Immune Response

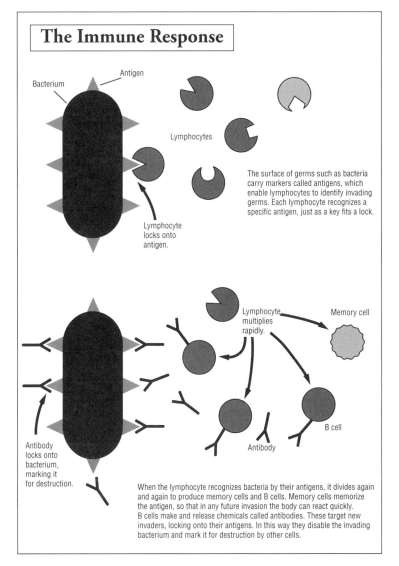

Bacterium

Antigen

Lymphocytes

The surface of germs such as bacteria carry markers called antigens, which enable lymphocytes to identify invading germs. Each lymphocyte recognizes a specific antigen, just as a key fits a lock.

Lymphocyte locks onto antigen.

Lymphocyte multiplies rapidly.

Memory cell

B cell

Antibody

Antibody locks onto bacterium, marking it for destruction.

When the lymphocyte recognizes bacteria by their antigens, it divides again and again to produce memory cells and B cells. Memory cells memorize the antigen, so that in any future invasion the body can react quickly. B cells make and release chemicals called antibodies. These target new invaders, locking onto their antigens. In this way they disable the invading bacterium and mark it for destruction by other cells.

smallpox called ingrafting. No one knows how it was developed, but over time, a treatment was devised where pus from the sore of a person with a mild case of smallpox was smeared into a scratch on the arm of a healthy person. The person who was ingrafted usually developed mild symptoms but recovered quickly. They never caught smallpox again.

This technique spread to Europe with the help of Lady Mary Wortley Montagu, the wife of the British ambassador living in Turkey in 1716. After witnessing this procedure, she had her three-year-old son ingrafted. She brought news of the technique back to England, where it was called inoculation. The procedure was not widely used because, although it was successful, there was a risk that the patient could develop a severe case of the disease.

The First Vaccine

One boy who was inoculated was eight-year-old Edward Jenner. He survived the painful procedure and grew up to be a country doctor whose keen observations led to the first vaccinations.

In 1796 Jenner noticed that young women who milked cows sometimes became infected with cowpox, a disease that caused sores on a cow's udders. The girls would get painful sores on their hands, but the disease was not fatal. Once the girls caught cowpox, they never became infected with smallpox.

In May of that year Jenner performed his first cow-pox experiment. He took fluid from a sore on the hand of dairymaid Sarah Nelmes and inoculated a healthy eight-year-old boy named James Phipps. Within a few days James came down with a fever and a small sore. On July 1, believing that the cowpox inoculation would prevent the development of smallpox, Jenner inoculated James with matter from a smallpox patient. Nineteen days later Jenner wrote, "The Boy has since been inoculated for the Smallpox which as I ventured to predict produced no effects. I shall now pursue my Experiments with redoubled ardor."[15]

Jenner went on to repeat his experiments and published his results, calling his technique vaccination and the matter taken from the cowpox sore a vaccine (derived from *vacca*, the Latin word for cow). In a letter written to a friend, Jenner predicted, "The annihilation of smallpox—the most dreadful scourge of the human race—will be the final result of this practice."[16] Jenner would never know how accurate his prediction would become. He also would never know how his vaccine worked or even what kind of organism he was actually fighting against. That information would not come for many more years.

How Vaccines Work

Vaccines work by using our own natural defenses. An injection of a weakened virus or a part of a virus is just enough to trigger the lymphocytes to create memory cells. If the virus invades again, the body is able to fight it with ready-made antibodies before a serious infection takes hold. Vaccines may be made with dead microbes or parts of dead viruses. Some are made with living microbes that are weakened and rendered harmless but are still able to elicit an immune response.

Rabies Vaccine

Louis Pasteur had created a successful vaccine for chickens, another for sheep, and he had been experimenting on a rabies vaccine for dogs, but he had not developed a safe vaccine for humans. But that did not matter to the mother of nine-year-old Joseph Meister, who took her son to Pasteur's office in 1885. A mad dog had bitten Joseph. Rabies is a horrible disease that infects only mammals. The virus attacks the nervous system and infects the brain, causing a difficult and painful death.

Pasteur knew that a weakened germ worked as a vaccine against other diseases in animals and believed that a similar treatment for humans should work against rabies. He injected Joseph with the weakened vaccine and increased the dose daily. After fourteen days Joseph Meister was stronger and had made history. He became the first person to survive rabies.

More Vaccines

Pasteur's success inspired a concerted effort to develop vaccines for other dreadful diseases, but it did not happen quickly. Max Theiler created a vaccine against yellow

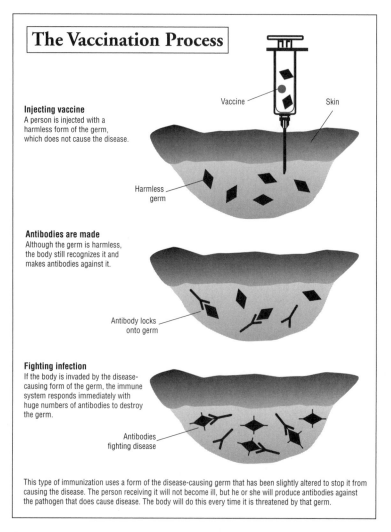

The Vaccination Process

Injecting vaccine
A person is injected with a harmless form of the germ, which does not cause the disease.

Vaccine

Skin

Harmless germ

Antibodies are made
Although the germ is harmless, the body still recognizes it and makes antibodies against it.

Antibody locks onto germ

Fighting infection
If the body is invaded by the disease-causing form of the germ, the immune system responds immediately with huge numbers of antibodies to destroy the germ.

Antibodies fighting disease

This type of immunization uses a form of the disease-causing germ that has been slightly altered to stop it from causing the disease. The person receiving it will not become ill, but he or she will produce antibodies against the pathogen that does cause disease. The body will do this every time it is threatened by that germ.

fever in the 1920s, and Jonas Salk and Albert Sabin produced polio vaccines in the 1950s.

Today, there are vaccines for mumps, rubella, measles, tetanus, chicken pox, flu, and other once dangerous diseases. But there are many viral infections that the medical community cannot prevent with an injection. For example, there are too many strains of the common cold to create an effective vaccine, and other viruses mutate too quickly. A virus can alter its outer protein coat so that antibodies and vaccines that once worked on the virus are no longer effective. Even a slight difference can mean that a person's memory cells would not recognize the virus, and the antibodies that a person's immune system created in the past would be powerless against this new strain.

The First Antibiotics

It seems ironic that medical researchers were successful in developing a preventive medicine for viruses, which were unknown to science and unseen by man, but were not able to fight off known bacterial infections. The key was finding a way to kill a bacterium cell without harming human cells.

The first breakthrough came in 1910, when Paul Ehrlich, a German scientist, discovered that an arsenic compound killed a spiral-shaped bacterium called a spirochete that caused syphilis. His discovery was inspired by Robert Koch's work with aniline dye. In a meeting in Berlin, Ehrlich heard Koch describe how he used the dye to identify the tuberculosis bacterium. When Koch applied the dye, it stained the bacteria cells, making them easier to see under a microscope, but it also killed the microbes.

Ehrlich experimented with many other dyes and chemical compounds before he achieved success with arsenic compound 606, which was dubbed "the magic bullet."

How Antibiotics Work

Ehrlich's compound was called a magic bullet because, like other antibiotic agents, it specifically targeted the syphilis spirochete. Antibiotics are simply chemicals that react with other chemicals. Every cell, whether it is human or bacterium, is also made up of chemicals. The cell's membranes are covered with receptor sites that allow the cell to react with or take in other chemicals. In order for an antibiotic to work, it must have the right chemical makeup, or key, to fit the chemical makeup, or lock, at the receptor site on the bacterium. But the antibiotic's chemical key must not fit the receptor sites of other cells in the patient's body. If it does, then it would cause adverse side effects.

Each kind of antibiotic attacks a bacterium in a different way. Some, like penicillin, stop the bacteria from forming a cell wall. Other antibiotics interfere with the bacteria's ability to make essential nutrients, such as folic acid and other proteins, while others stop the bacteria's DNA replication.

Penicillin

The power of microorganisms can be harnessed to heal as well as harm. This was discovered by chance when Alexander Fleming observed a yellowish mold growing on a bacterial culture in his lab. It was 1928, and Fleming had been studying staphylococcus, which is a common bacterium on skin. He noticed that wherever the mold grew, an area of clear liquid surrounding it was free of bacteria. Wherever Fleming spread the mold juice, which Fleming called penicillin, bacterial growth was stopped dead. Although penicillin worked wonders, Fleming was unable to present it to the public. Apparently people were not ready to accept a microorganism that could make an effective antibiotic.

Twelve years later, a young Australian doctor named Howard Walter Florey, along with his colleagues Ernst Boris Chain and Dr. Norman G. Heatley, showed the world that penicillin was indeed a miracle drug. It killed the bacteria that caused scarlet fever, pneumonia, diphtheria, and meningitis, as well as other common bacterial infections.

The discovery of penicillin was so important that American soldiers were sent to collect soil samples from India, China, Africa, and South America so that it could be tested for other miracle molds. Employees of the U.S. Department of Agriculture laboratory in Peoria, Illinois, were instructed to collect any unusual molds as well. One employee, Mary Hunt, earned the nickname Moldy Mary because she searched through peo-

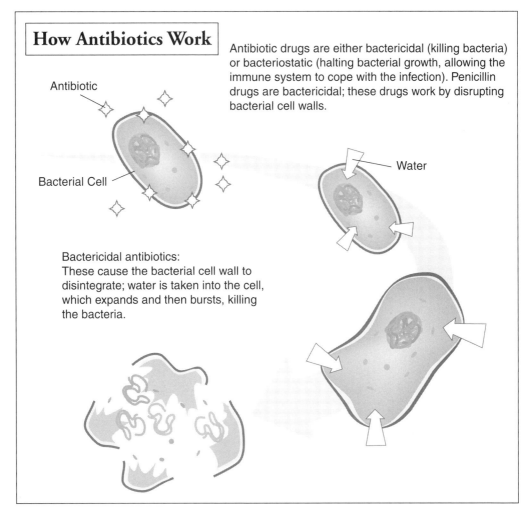

How Antibiotics Work

Antibiotic drugs are either bactericidal (killing bacteria) or bacteriostatic (halting bacterial growth, allowing the immune system to cope with the infection). Penicillin drugs are bactericidal; these drugs work by disrupting bacterial cell walls.

Antibiotic

Bacterial Cell

Water

Bactericidal antibiotics:
These cause the bacterial cell wall to disintegrate; water is taken into the cell, which expands and then bursts, killing the bacteria.

ple's garbage cans and litter. While poking through a neighbor's trash, Mary found a rotting cantaloupe that had a golden mold growing on it. When the melon mold was tested, it produced twice as much penicillin as Fleming's mold, and it grew easily in large quantities. It was named *Penicillium chrysogenum,* and it replaced Fleming's mold for use in penicillin production until researchers learned to make the drug synthetically.

Drugs Dug from the Earth

Every pharmaceutical company raced to find new antibiotic compounds. Bristol-Meyers Pharmaceuticals

In the wake of Alexander Fleming's discovery of penicillin in 1928, the U.S. Department of Agriculture discovered that mold growing on rotting fruit produces large amounts of the antibiotic.

sent envelopes to all of its stockholders with instructions to collect soil samples from their neighborhoods. Other companies contacted missionaries in far-off places, foreign news correspondents, airline pilots, and deep-sea divers in their search for a mold that might lead to a new treatment.

In 1943 Dr. Paul Burkholder at Yale University sent out plastic mailing tubes to everyone he knew and received more than seven thousand soil samples in return. One soil sample sent from Venezuela contained a powerful antibiotic that was eventually developed into the drug called Chloromycetin. It killed many different kinds of microbes, including the deadly bacteria that caused Rocky Mountain spotted fever and typhus.

Dr. Selman Waksman at Rutgers University worked for the pharmaceutical firm Merck & Company. He tested the mold found in the throat of a New Jersey chicken. It contained a compound called streptomycin that killed the tuberculosis bacillus—something penicillin could not do.

Man over Microbes

With the development of antibiotics, common infectious diseases lost their grip on the world. People believed that man had conquered harmful bacteria and viruses. The medical community even fulfilled Jenner's prediction of annihilating smallpox.

By the end of the 1800s, many European countries had enacted laws requiring its citizens to be vaccinated against smallpox. In short order, the virus disappeared from many countries. Surprisingly one of the last Western countries to eradicate smallpox from within its borders was the United States, in the late 1940s.

The success of mandatory vaccination inspired officials at the United Nations to adopt a resolution to eradicate smallpox from the forty-four countries that still reported its occurrence. The World Health Organization (WHO), which is part of the United Nations, set a deadline of January 1, 1977.

Teams of medical workers searched for outbreaks of smallpox in poor pockets of major cities and remote villages. Wherever an outbreak occurred, the team swooped in to vaccinate all the inhabitants, creating a ring of containment around the victims in a particular area. Those who were infected were put into quarantine. Defusing each epidemic case by case and country by country, the WHO successfully snuffed out the once raging flames of smallpox.

By 1979 the WHO declared the project a success. The only places on Earth where smallpox existed were in laboratory test tubes. One question remained: What should be done with the stored virus? Some nations voluntarily destroyed their supplies, and others handed them over to research centers in the Soviet Union or

A Nigerian woman receives a smallpox vaccination in 1969 during the World Health Organization's effort to wipe out smallpox. By 1979 the virus had been eradicated.

the United States. There are now about four hundred vials of frozen virus securely stored at the U.S. Centers for Disease Control in Atlanta, Georgia, and another two hundred stored in a lab in Moscow. Although the WHO ordered the destruction of all smallpox samples in 1993, the order was not carried out. Scientists still debate the validity of destroying a virus species. Some argue that more study could provide clues to fighting other deadly microbes.

Fighting Back

The elimination of smallpox and the availability of so many antibiotics lulled the world into believing that infectious diseases were a thing of the past. The U.S. surgeon general William H. Steward even declared before Congress in 1969 that he was ready to "close the book"[17] on infectious disease. The development of antibiotics was put on the back burner.

But as quickly as man could manufacture antibiotics and vaccines, bacteria and viruses were faster to develop resistance to the drugs. In an interview with *Newsweek,* Dr. Richard Wenzel of the University of Iowa said, "Ever since 1928, when Alexander Fleming discovered penicillin, man and microbe have been in a footrace. Right now the microorganisms are winning. They're so much older than we are . . . and wiser."[18]

Microbes Mutate

The wisdom of a microbe lies in its ability to change. They are able to reproduce much faster than their human competitors. A new generation can come along as quickly as every fifteen minutes, and each time a bacterium divides, there is a chance for error. A random change in the genetic makeup of a cell that becomes a permanent inherited characteristic is called a mutation. And a mutation that increases a microbe's chance of survival is passed on to the next generation.

Bacteria can also trade or share parts of their DNA through a process called horizontal gene transfer. In addition to strands of DNA, bacteria have rings of DNA called plasmids. These plasmids give the bacteria certain survival skills, such as being resistant to a type of antibiotic. This means that bacteria in the same generation can potentially share advantageous plasmids, just as easily as two friends exchange phone numbers. Two bacteria can exchange a gene or genes that allow them to inhabit a new species of animal, thrive in a new climate, or protect them against a certain drug.

Growing Resistance

The use of antibiotics creates a situation in which the fittest microbes survive. Each time someone uses an antibiotic, the majority of the bacteria are killed but not all. These heartier microbes are left to multiply and spread their resistance to the next generation. Within four years of the widespread use of penicillin in the 1940s, doctors saw evidence of microbes that had grown resistant to it. Even Alexander Fleming himself warned the public in a *New York Times* interview of the dangers of taking antibiotics. "The microbes are educated to resist penicillin and a host of penicillin-fast [resistant] organisms is bred out which can be passed to other individuals and from them to others until they reach someone who gets a septicemia or a pneumonia which penicillin cannot save."[19]

As each new antibiotic came on the market, a microbe came along that could withstand the toxic effects. Today doctors are encouraged to stop prescribing antibiotics for viral infections, because they have no power over a virus. And when patients are prescribed an antibiotic, they need to take the entire dose. After two days on an antibiotic, a patient usually starts to feel better, but that is only because the antibiotic has killed off a significant number of bacteria. The minute treatment is stopped, the surviving bacteria begin to multiply. It takes only one drug-resistant bacterium to multiply into millions.

The Bacteria Eaters

One treatment that may prove to be a solution to the problem of antibiotic resistance comes from an unlikely source—viruses. It is a method developed in Russia before Fleming discovered penicillin. To modern mentality it seems bizarre, for it pits microbes against each other.

Phage therapy harnesses specific kinds of viruses that attack only certain harmful bacteria. Discovered and named by Felix d'Herelle in 1917, bacteriophages (bacteria-eating viruses) were soon used by doctors to

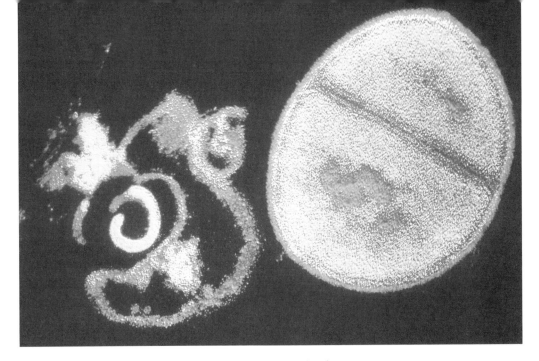

cure cholera and typhoid fever. Although the treatment never caught on in the West, research continues, particularly in the Republic of Georgia. Today the world's foremost center for the development of phage therapy is at the Eliava Institute in Tbilisi, Georgia. Doctors at the institute study a wide range of viruses collected from nature. The viruses that are active against harmful bacteria are then cultivated and used for treatment. A patient suffering from an antibiotic-resistant bacterial infection is injected with a solution that contains the proper bacteriophages. The viruses seek out the larger harmful bacteria and inject their genetic material into the cell, where it hijacks the bacteria's reproductive machinery. Only one hundred bacteriophages placed on an infected wound is enough to destroy more than 100 million bacteria. Once the bacteria are eliminated, the viruses also die out. They have no cells to infect and are washed harmlessly out of the patient's body.

More than twenty companies in the United States are now studying and testing phage therapy in the lab and will seek future government approval to conduct clinical trials on humans. In the meantime, dozens of exotic, mysterious illnesses are cropping up all over the world.

Staphylococcus bacteria are destroyed by antibiotics. Although antibiotics are extremely effective, their use over time results in heartier, drug-resistant strains of bacteria.

Chapter 4

Emerging Microbes

Many infectious diseases, like smallpox, polio, and anthrax, are ancient and have plagued humankind for thousands of years. But new strains of bacteria and viruses continue to emerge seemingly out of nowhere to cause mysterious new ailments.

In Wisconsin in May 2003, three-year-old Schyan Kautzer came down with symptoms vaguely reminiscent of smallpox. Eileen Whitmarsh, a forty-two-year-old pet store owner, developed flulike symptoms along with blisters on her head and under her arms. Two employees at a veterinary clinic also became sick. The one thing they all had in common was a close encounter with prairie dogs. The three-year-old had received a prairie dog for a pet, the pet store owner had had the animals in stock, and the workers at the clinic had recently treated a sick prairie dog.

Blood samples taken from all the victims revealed startling news: They had a disease never encountered before in the Western Hemisphere—a virus called monkeypox, a less severe cousin to smallpox. At one time the virus infected only rodents in Africa, but it had jumped species and was now known to have infected fewer than one hundred people in Africa. But how did it travel five thousand miles across an ocean to a small town in Wisconsin?

A Global Village

Microbes are opportunists. They take advantage of likely and unlikely hosts. The virus that was carried to the United States inside an African rodent seized the opportunity to inhabit a new species when the animal was housed in a small, tightly packed cage next to prairie dogs in a pet store warehouse. The virus mutated, or changed its genetic code, so that it was able to infect a new species. From a Gambian rat to an American prairie dog, it then jumped to a little girl.

Crowded cities and the ease of intercontinental travel facilitate the spread of microbes throughout the world.

Humans live in a global society, and our actions affect the microscopic community around us. "We do things as part of progress, which we don't recognize as changing the microbial environment,"[20] says G. Richard Olds, the chairman of medicine at the Medical College of Wisconsin and the former head of the Tropical Disease and Travel Medicine Center in New England. Everything a person does affects the microscopic world: traveling in airplanes, eating foreign foods, and living in crowded cities. As Olds says, "Nothing happens on this planet that doesn't impact us. We're wearing clothes that were made in China. We're eating foods that were grown in Chile."[21] Infective agents can come from anywhere, and frequently do. Monkeypox appeared in this country because of people's passion for exotic pets.

But the connection between man and microbe was not always so apparent. Disease was something that just happened to a person, and there was little thought as to why or how a person's behavior or activities contributed to their illness. It took hundreds of years before someone thought to look at our own behavior and modify it in an attempt to prevent the spread of disease.

The First Disease Detective

In 1854, during the Industrial Revolution, living conditions in many parts of urban England were poor. Factories belched black smoke, and slums were overcrowded and unsanitary—the perfect conditions for bacteria and viruses. An outbreak of cholera occurred in a small area near Broad Street in London. Cholera is contracted by drinking water infected with the cholera bacterium or eating food contaminated by it. Cholera causes severe diarrhea, vomiting, fever, and death.

When physician John Snow began questioning people in the neighborhood, he noticed that of the seventy-seven households infected with cholera, fifty-nine used the hand pump on Broad Street. Families that remained healthy used a water pump farther away.

Near the Broad Street well was a cesspool that contained the waste and garbage of the neighborhood. Snow believed that sewage from the cesspool had contaminated the drinking water. He begged the board of trustees of the St. James Parish to remove the handle from the pump to prevent people from collecting the contaminated water. Although no other physician agreed with Snow's assessment, the men on the board did as he advised. The handle was removed and the cases of cholera declined. Later Snow learned that the bricks lining the cesspool were indeed old and broken, and sewage had leaked into the well.

Disease Detectives Today

The same kind of detective work that Snow conducted in the 1800s is carried out today by scientists at the Centers for Disease Control and Prevention (CDC) headquartered in Atlanta, Georgia, and the Division for Emerging and Other Communicable Diseases Surveillance and Control at the World Health Organization (WHO). More properly called epidemiologists, these scientists study the spread of infectious illnesses and respond to outbreaks anywhere in the world.

They watch for the emergence of a new disease or an old microbial adversary using a network of doctors and high-tech equipment like satellites and the Internet. The WHO is continuously monitoring the World Wide Web with a customized search engine called the Global Public Health Intelligence Network, listening for rumors and reports of suspicious disease-related events. Online eavesdropping led to the early detection of the 2003 outbreak of SARS (severe acute respiratory syndrome).

When a suspicious event is detected or when epidemiologists are consulted by local authorities, these scientists use some of the same skills that police detectives use when trying to solve a crime. They interview the patients, their friends, and family to pinpoint the initial signs of illness. They ask patients what they may have eaten, what animals or animal products they may have come in contact with, and where they may have traveled. As each person is interviewed, patterns of the disease emerge. Are the victims all children, or are they all adults? Are they mostly male or female? Knowing when an outbreak began, who it affected, and when it ended gives epidemiologists an idea of the kind of disease that could have occurred within that time frame.

Epidemiologists also track each patient's activities to narrow down the possible source of infection and plot each incident on a map to see if there is a geographical element. They search the area for evidence of animal activity, insects, or contaminated water or food. Doctors take samples of blood or tissue and send them to their lab in Georgia, where microbiologists will identify the microbes involved in the incident.

Epidemiologists from the World Health Organization conduct research on the Ebola virus. Epidemiologists study the incidence, spread, and control of infectious diseases.

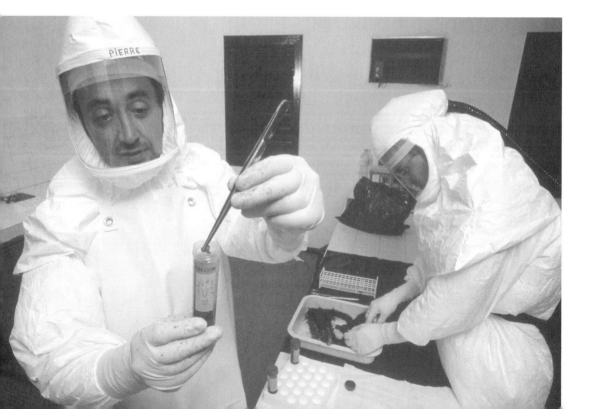

Suspect infectious agents are examined in a lab called a biocontainment unit. There are four levels of security and safety features in the labs. The most deadly infectious agents are examined in biocontainment unit level 4, which is as airtight as a space shuttle. Air locks and a ventilation system that sucks air inward prevent dangerous bacteria or viruses from drifting out. Microbiologists suit up in astronaut-like "blue suits" complete with their own air supply. At the end of the day, the workers are decontaminated in chemical showers. The evidence found in the lab combined with the information gathered in the field will lead to the cause and hopefully the treatment of the infection.

Microbes on the Move

Epidemiologists respond to outbreaks all around the world, but today our world is more mobile than ever before, and that mobility means that microbes are on the move too. "One of the most important means of spreading diseases around the globe is air travel,"[22] says David Heymann, the director of communicable diseases for the World Health Organization.

Every day, more than 500 million people travel across international borders, and tens of billions of bacteria and viruses hitch a ride. In 2003, within six months of the first reported case of SARS in China, the disease was spread by air travel to twenty-seven other countries. All the victims who came down with SARS in Toronto, Canada, could be traced directly back to one woman who had traveled from Hong Kong. And shortly after the Toronto outbreak, the World Health Organization warned travelers not to visit the city and effectively prevented the virus from spreading further.

Changing the Environment

People not only get around faster than ever before, but they change the environment more easily too.

Every day, in some part of the world, whole tracts of rain forests are bulldozed, rivers are dammed, and new roads are paved into the wilderness. This disrupts the balance and distribution of plants and animals, including microbes. It may cut off a virus from its host so that the virus must seek another means of survival.

The story of Lyme disease, which causes arthritis-like aches and pains, provides an example of this process. In the 1800s settlers in Old Lyme, Connecticut, clear-cut the old growth forests, which led to a decline in the deer population. A hundred years later, when the agricultural production in that area ceased, the forests returned, along with a burgeoning deer population. But the human population grew too. Housing developments in forested areas put man, deer, and microbes on a collision course.

The spirochete *Borrelia burgdorferi* is passed from a deer to a deer mouse by the bite of an infected deer tick. The deer and the deer mouse do not seem particularly affected by the microbe, but people are. When people started to build houses in Old Lyme, they unwittingly placed themselves in the path of the microbe and added a new host to the microbe's list.

Even making more subtle changes to the landscape—such as digging pools, opening irrigation ditches, and discarding tires—create new niches for vectors, animals that are capable of carrying human disease. Insects carry about one hundred different human diseases, which are called arboviruses (*ar*thropod-*bo*rne viruses). Topping the list are yellow fever, dengue fever, malaria, and West Nile virus.

West Nile Virus

In the summer of 1999 the New York City Health Department battled a mysterious outbreak of encephalitis (inflammation of the brain) among a group of elderly people living near LaGuardia Airport. Tests revealed that it was West Nile virus, a disease never before seen outside of the Middle East.

The virus is carried by mosquitoes that take advantage of hot, wet summers in urban and suburban areas. "West Nile is extraordinarily good at adapting to this new environment,"[23] said Ian Lipkin, director of the Jerome L. and Dawn Greene Infectious Disease Laboratory at Columbia University. Mosquitoes lay infected eggs in puddles, pools, overturned toys, garbage cans, and any other place rainwater can accumulate.

Deer ticks like this one can carry Lyme disease, a viral infection that causes arthritis-like aches and pains.

West Nile usually infects birds. People living in the suburbs of Chicago, one of the most heavily hit areas, reported an eerie silence where once songbirds trilled and crows cawed. No one knows why or how it got to the United States, but this versatile virus managed to quickly jump species once it arrived. It is now known to infect dozens of bird species, as well as humans, horses, chipmunks, squirrels, raccoons, bats, rare rhinoceroses in zoos, and wild alligators. These animals are only innocent bystanders in the virus's life cycle.

In order to cause disease, a mosquito must first bite an infected bird and pick up the virus, which ends up in the digestive tract of the mosquito, where it multiplies. While other arboviruses are carried inside the gut of only one or two species of insect, the West Nile virus has been found living in thirty-six different species of mosquito. The virus spreads throughout the mosquito's body, ending up in the salivary glands. When the mosquito bites its next victim, the virus is injected into the new host along with mosquito saliva.

In the short time since West Nile virus first appeared, scientists have learned a great deal about it. The virus's ability to replicate is closely related to the weather. At 70 degrees Fahrenheit, it takes the virus three weeks to multiply to a point where it is transferable to another animal. At 80 degrees Fahrenheit, the time is shortened to two weeks, and during spells with temperatures higher than 90 degrees Fahrenheit, it takes only one week. The hotter the weather, the more infectious the disease becomes. This information is not just interesting virus trivia; it is vital data that allows health officials to predict the severity of an outbreak by monitoring the weather. If a large outbreak is predicted, then officials may spray insecticides and issue health warnings to residents in the area. But even with early warnings, the dis-

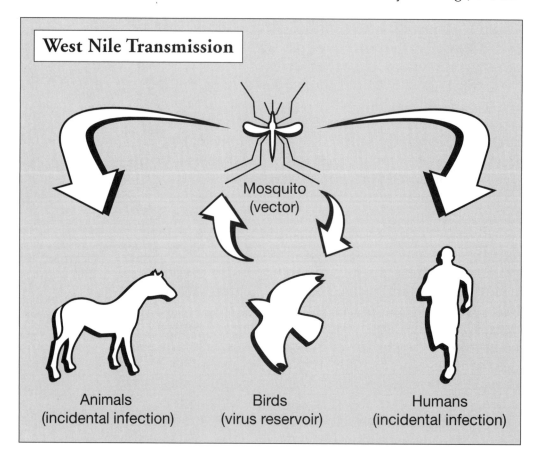

West Nile Transmission

Mosquito
(vector)

Animals
(incidental infection)

Birds
(virus reservoir)

Humans
(incidental infection)

ease is spreading. At the end of 1999, the CDC reported that sixty-two people had been infected in four states and seven people had died. Within three years, the virus had spread to forty-four states, reporting 4,156 cases of illness and 284 deaths.

Hidden Danger

Some infectious diseases are spread by animals, while others are passed directly from person to person. Some may sweep through a population like wildfire, while others lurk and linger.

In the summer of 1981, five men in Los Angeles were hospitalized with weakened immune systems and uncontrolled rare infections and tumors. Not long afterward, similar cases were reported in New York, San Francisco, and Newark, New Jersey. By the end of the year, 150 cases of the illness had been reported and thirty people were dead. This was the first slow appearance of what would later be called human immunodeficiency virus (HIV), which causes AIDS (acquired immunodeficiency syndrome). After years of study, researchers discovered that this RNA retrovirus might have made its first appearance in the human population as early as 1959, perhaps even earlier. HIV is capable of hiding out within a person's cells for up to twenty years before the symptoms of AIDS develop. Like other viruses, HIV targets one particular kind of cell, but the reason that HIV is so deadly is that it attacks the immune system's white blood cells. By entering and killing only those cells, the virus kills the cells that allow the body to protect itself against other infectious diseases.

Hiding out inside a person's cells for years is an effective way for the virus to survive. It can be passed from person to person long before any signs of illness appear. HIV can spread through having contact with blood and other bodily fluids from an infected person, engaging in sexual activity with an infected person, sharing a contaminated hypodermic needle, and

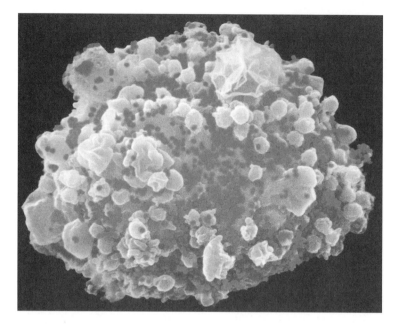

An electron micrograph shows a T cell infected with the HIV virus. The virus can lie dormant in the human body for years before it develops into AIDS.

receiving a blood transfusion. It may also be passed from an infected mother to her fetus during pregnancy.

As one of the smallest viruses, measuring only .1 micron in size, HIV has caused as much devastation in the African continent as smallpox did in the New World five hundred years ago. In Zimbabwe and other African countries, one out of every five adults is infected. But the virus is also a worldwide epidemic. The WHO reported that at the end of 2003 an estimated 40 million people across the globe lived with HIV, and the disease AIDS had taken the lives of 25 million. With no vaccine and very few effective long-term treatments, AIDS continues to take the lives of 3 million people every year.

Biological Warfare and Terrorism

It would seem that the CDC and the WHO have enough on their plate just monitoring and responding to natural outbreaks of disease, but they also respond to acts of bioterrorism—the use of a biological substance like a bacteria or a virus as a weapon. Bioterrorism is a concept nearly as old as war itself. Greek and Roman armies threw dead and bloating animals into their enemy's water supplies to make them sick. In 1763 British officers gave gifts of smallpox-infected blankets to un-suspecting Native American chiefs. For decades many nations, including the United States, experimented with microbes as weapons until the ratification of the Bacteriological and Toxic Weapons Convention in 1972. But evidence suggests that some countries and terror-ist groups still have active biological warfare programs.

The list of potential bacterial and viral weapons is short but deadly. The microbes most likely to be used for an attack are those that are highly lethal, easily produced in large quantities, and easily transmittable. Anthrax tops the list, because it can be collected from soil samples or illegally acquired from germ banks. It can be contracted through the skin or ingested. It at-tacks the body and shuts down the immune system. Inhaling anthrax is almost always fatal.

Each year the U.S. federal government responds to hun-dreds of anthrax hoaxes, but on October 5, 2001, it was the real thing. On that day began a series of biological

FBI agents work to decontaminate a Florida building targeted during the anthrax terrorist attacks of October 2001.

terrorist attacks in which envelopes containing high-grade anthrax were sent to addresses in Florida, New Jersey, New York, and Washington, D.C. Seventeen people were taken ill, and five people died. The attacks shut down the postal service and other government agencies for several days, costing the nation millions of dollars.

The botulin bacterium has also been used as a weapon because it produces one of the most toxic chemicals known, but it cannot be as effectively distributed. In 1984 members of the Rajneesh cult in Oregon sprinkled the bacteria on restaurant salad bars in an attempt to affect the outcome of an upcoming local election. The Oregon incident injured more than seven hundred citizens but did not cause any fatalities.

The smallpox virus is another cause for concern. When the virus was eradicated from nature, there was no need to continue the vaccination program, so today very few people have a natural immunity to fight the disease. It would spread easily through a population. In 2002, in the wake of the World Trade Center attack and the anthrax incidents, President George W. Bush announced reinstating a voluntary smallpox vaccination program for frontline health-care workers and first responders and a mandatory vaccination program for military personnel.

Investigations have uncovered that microbes like smallpox or anthrax can be obtained illegally from unregulated labs and former storehouses. No one knows how many deadly germs are available or easily obtainable, but according to the World Federation for Culture Collections, there are forty-six registered germ banks that contain anthrax, and there are more than one thousand that are not registered or regulated.

These germ banks are like microbial libraries where legitimate scientists can request specimens of certain bacteria or viruses for research purposes. They hold more than just dangerous pathogens. Germ banks also contain an assortment of other bacteria and virus cultures that are experimented with and used for more positive purposes.

Chapter 5

Harnessing Invisible Power

For centuries people have been using microbes to their advantage, turning grapes into wine, milk into cheese, and cabbage into sauerkraut. People benefit from what microbes do naturally: They eat. They digest organic compounds, changing the chemical makeup of one product and turning it into a completely different yet tasty food or drink.

Milk, for example, is turned into cottage cheese when the bacteria *Leuconostoc* break down the milk sugar (lactose) to produce lactic acid. The acid curdles the milk into cheese curds. Different types of bacteria or mold make different kinds of cheeses.

Bacteria are used in the production of all kinds of foods. Before coffee beans are washed, dried, and roasted, they are first soaked in a tank of bacteria that break down bits of shell still stuck on the bean. And without microbes, there would be no chocolate. Cocoa beans must first be fermented by bacteria and yeast before they become edible.

Louis Pasteur described the fermentation process more than one hundred years ago as the addition of a living organism such as a bacteria or yeast to another substance. Under anaerobic conditions (where no oxygen is present), the bacteria break down the carbohydrates and produce alcohol and carbon dioxide. For centuries this process has resulted in wine, beer, bread, and other good things to eat.

Genetic Engineering

Today, in order to get bacteria to produce a desired product, they are first altered through a process called genetic engineering. Bacteria are useful because their strands of DNA float loosely in the cell, making them easy to get at. They also have several plasmid rings that give a cell resistance to certain chemicals and determine what kind of materials it can break down and use for food or what enzymes it can make. Once a gene is identified, it can be taken out and inserted into another bacterium.

Genetic engineers have devised two ways to insert genetic information into a cell. One way is to use an RNA retrovirus as a vector. Just as an animal or insect vector carries a disease from person to person, a virus can be used to carry genes from one cell to another.

First the scientists must remove any harmful parts of the virus so that it will not cause disease. The desired gene or genes are then inserted inside the virus. When the virus infects the appropriate cell, the cell copies the virus's RNA, incorporating the bits of genetic information into its own DNA. Virus vectors are used to modify plants and are being experimented with for use in gene therapy for genetic disorders.

But the tool that is most commonly used in industrial genetic engineering is the bacterial plasmid, which is used to insert new genes the same way that bacteria exchange genetic information naturally. Special enzymes cut the plasmid at specific locations, opening up the DNA at precise points. A gene is taken out and replaced by a new gene that will give the bacteria the desired characteristic. It is inserted back into the plasmid and "glued" in place with another enzyme. The engineered plasmid is then reinserted back into the bacterium.

Each time the bacterium divides, the engineered plasmid is duplicated as well. When trillions of these bacteria contain the altered genes, they become powerful minifactories producing much-needed products.

A pharmaceutical technician works with a bioreactor. Bioreactors house millions of engineered microbes that produce the basic building blocks of a wide variety of products.

Microbial Factories

Engineered microbes are a cheap labor force. They do not take up much space or eat a lot. Massive quantities of bacteria can be grown in bioreactors—enormous stainless-steel vats several stories high, filled with a nutrient-rich substance to keep the bacteria productive. In this kind of environment bacteria churn out acids, proteins, and enzymes that are used to manufacture a whole host of products.

Using engineered microbes in an industrial setting is called bioprocessing. The first step is finding the appropriate microbe for the job and the perfect living conditions for the microbe's maximum production. A slight change in the temperature, concentration of nutrients, or level of oxygen inside the vat may diminish the bacteria's productivity.

One of the first uses of microbes in industry was the manufacture of vitamins that are added to foods or made into supplements. Many vitamins can be synthesized or made by combining certain chemicals in a lab, but others have far more complicated molecular structures. Humans normally depend on microbes to manufacture these vitamins for them as they digest food in the intestines. In the manufacturing world, bacteria are also depended on to create these essential compounds. The bacterium *Bacillus subtilis* is used to produce the much-needed vitamin called riboflavin, which is used by all living cells to create certain proteins. The bacterium secretes the riboflavin through its cell membrane. Once free of the bacteria, the riboflavin must be separated from the growth medium. This can be done by spinning it in a centrifuge or distilling it out. Manufactured riboflavin is added to cereals, bread, and other fortified foods.

The bacterium *Lactobacillus bulgaricus* makes lactic acid, which is used not only to preserve and ferment foods but also to dissolve lacquers on furniture and remove hair from cowhides before they are tanned into leather. *Aspergillus niger* produces vast quantities of citric acid, which is used in soft drinks, candies, inks, and Alka-Seltzer. The *Bacillus subtilis* bacterium is also genetically altered to produce protease, an enzyme that is added to meat tenderizers, drain cleaners, liquid glue, and laundry detergent.

High-fructose corn syrup that sweetens most soft drinks is also made with bacteria. Cornstarch is treated with a series of three enzymes to convert its sucrose into fructose, which is twice as sweet and therefore cheaper to use. The enzymes used in the process are made by bacteria.

By genetically altering a bacterium's DNA and inserting a human gene, scientists can program a bacterium to produce a human protein. The gene for making human insulin, for example, is inserted into the bacterium's chromosomes so that it begins to churn out vast amounts of insulin that is needed by people who suffer from diabetes. Other strains of bacteria have been programmed to make human growth hormone and a vaccine for hoof-and-mouth disease. Every day, researchers work on ways that bacterium can manufacture more drugs and hormones to treat other medical problems.

Feeding the World

Genetically altered bacteria and viruses are also used in agriculture. Originally, genetic engineering techniques worked well only with animal cells, because plants have tough cell walls that most bacteria can not get through. And those that can are usually harmful. But scientists found a way to take a harmful bacterium called *Agrobacterium tumifaciens,* which normally causes crown gall disease, and make it beneficial. The bacterium infects a plant by inserting its DNA into the plant cell, which causes a tumor to grow. But when the disease-causing gene is snipped out of the bacterium's plasmid, the bacterium is rendered harmless and becomes the perfect vector.

Viruses can also be used to modify plant genes. One such virus comes from the well-studied mosaic virus family, namely the cauliflower mosaic virus. It can be rendered harmless and fitted with genetic information that makes a plant more tolerant to herbicide or more insect resistant.

Genetically engineered foods are already on the market. Scientists have developed tomatoes that keep their fresh taste longer, peas that retain their sweetness, and strains of corn and wheat that are pest resistant. Some genetically modified potatoes contain 60 percent more starch. The extra starch decreases the amount of cooking oil that soaks into the potatoes, solving the problem of oily potato chips or greasy french fries. But more colorful tomatoes or greaseless chips are not the only reasons for this growing field of science.

Some scientists believe that genetically modified foods may be an important tool for feeding the world in the future. Researchers predict that we will need to increase global food production by 50 percent within the next fifty years in order to keep up with the population growth. That is a tall order to fill. So genetic engineers

Genetically altered bacteria and viruses are used to create disease-resistant plants that produce more food than unmodified plants.

are looking at ways to increase production; for example, developing plants that produce more food than they normally would or are able to fight off diseases that would otherwise diminish their yield.

But other scientists argue that genetically modified foods and plants are a cause for concern. They debate the safety and long-term effect that consuming modified foods will have on a person's health and the possible consequences of releasing genetically engineered recombinations into the environment. Mutations that may occur naturally within a plant will still occur within genetically modified cells. There is also the potential for naturally occurring viruses to recombine with the genetically altered viral DNA inserted into the plant. Could this cause a more virulent infection sometime in the future? As the debate continues, more than half of all food for sale in North America contains some form of genetically modified ingredients.

Biomining

The food and drug manufacturers are not the only industries that have used bacteria successfully. Another is the mining industry, which uses microbes to extract minerals from poor deposits of ore, a process dubbed biomining. The copper industry was the first to take advantage of these mini-miners. The bacterium *Thiobacillus ferooxidans* gets its energy by metabolizing inorganic materials. As the bacteria eat, they release a waste product of acid and an oxidizing solution of ferric ions. Together these wash the metal right out of the ore. The Romans first described this natural process two thousand years ago when they noticed that the runoff from a pile of leftover ore was blue with copper salts. The ancient miners found a way to recover the copper without ever knowing how it got there. The bacterium responsible for this phenomenon was not discovered until the 1960s. Today *T. ferooxidans* is used to extract more than 25 percent of all the copper mined in the world from what was once considered low-grade ore.

Gold ore, once thought to be useless for mining, is also releasing its gold deposits with the help of *T. ferooxidans*. A brew of microbes and fertilizer can be poured directly onto piles of crude ore. This method

Miners use microbes to extract minerals from poor deposits of ore, a process known as biomining.

is much cheaper, more efficient, and more environmentally friendly than other extraction processes.

So far the bacteria used in mining are collected from mining areas where they occur naturally. Because biomining has become so lucrative, the next step is to create super–mining microbes through genetic engineering to make them more efficient in the mining field. Once created, they could be mixed with microbes that can, for example, withstand extreme heat or resist toxic chemicals such as arsenic and mercury, which are used in processing gold.

There are so many different kinds of bacteria with so many different behaviors that scientists are always on the lookout for bacteria with unusual appetites and attributes. If one kind of bacteria can release gold from rock or turn sugar into alcohol, then perhaps another can turn wastewater into clean water.

Clean Water

The people of New York City produce 1.4 billion gallons of wastewater every day. Part of that—between 125 and 340 million gallons—is cleaned at the North River wastewater treatment plant on the Hudson River, which takes the sewage from Manhattan and cleans it with the help of bacteria. The wastewater is pumped into five thirty-foot-deep airing tanks that stimulate the growth of oxygen-loving bacteria. These microbes consume most of the organic materials or sludge in the wastewater. Then oxygen-hating (anaerobic) bacteria are used to clean the remaining sludge. In tanks called digesters, the sludge is heated to 95 degrees Fahrenheit to promote bacterial growth. As the bacteria eat the sludge, they produce methane gas. Instead of venting the methane out into the atmosphere, the gas is used to heat the digester tanks and run the other machinery at the sewage plant. Nothing is wasted, and the bacteria do most of the work.

The Oil Eaters

Other microbes are hard at work cleaning oil spills. In March 1989, when the *Exxon Valdez* oil tanker spilled

more than 11 million gallons of crude oil, it contaminated hundreds of miles of shoreline. Cleanup crews worked furiously to save the wildlife, but in the end, more than a quarter of a million birds, five thousand sea otters, and three hundred harbor seals lost their lives.

Within a few weeks, however, divers discovered that the most contaminated area in the ship's hold was thriving with sea life. Mother Nature had set out to repair herself. Naturally occurring bacteria in the water responded to the disaster and grew. They used the oil like food, changing the toxic petroleum into a harmless substance, a process that occurs only when other nutrients like nitrogen are present. Researchers learned from this discovery. Instead of washing away the oil from the shoreline with detergents that were harmful to the wildlife, they sprayed nitrogen onto the oil to encourage the growth of the oil-eating bacteria.

But cleaning that spill up was nothing compared to cleaning up the five hundred thousand tons of crude oil released into the water and soil surrounding the Mina Al-Ahmadi terminal during the 1990 Persian Gulf War. Newspapers around the world mourned the loss of plant and animal life in the region from the largest

Workers clean rocks after the 1989 Exxon Valdez *oil spill. During the cleanup, researchers learned that naturally occurring bacteria convert oil into a completely harmless substance.*

oil spill in history. Two years later, however, large mats of blue-green algae, or cyanobacteria, were growing on top of the oil-soaked soil. Embedded in the mats of cyanobacteria were millions of other bacteria, busy eating the oil and breaking it down into carbon and energy.

Researchers found a way to simulate these mats of microbes by using powdered clay sprinkled on the oil. The clay floated on the surface of the water and absorbed the oil, creating little islands where bacteria could float and feed. In one experiment, bacteria broke down three-quarters of a test spill in less than five weeks, a process that in nature would have taken closer to fifty years.

Bioremediation

In 1975 a massive leak at a military storage facility spilled eighty thousand gallons of kerosene-based jet fuel outside a quiet suburb of Charleston, South Carolina. Although the cleanup effort contained the spill, it could not prevent the fuel from seeping into groundwater. In less than ten years, highly toxic chemicals, such as cancer-causing benzene, had reached residential neighborhoods.

Studies conducted by the U.S. Geological Survey (USGS) found that microorganisms in the soil were actively consuming the toxic compounds. As they ate, they transformed the compounds into harmless carbon dioxide. By stimulating the bacteria with nutrients, the USGS team found they could increase the bacteria's activity. Through specially made infiltration systems, the nutrients were pumped into the contaminated soil. Tainted groundwater was filtered out and cleaned. In one year the contamination was reduced by 75 percent.

The process of using microbes as miniature cleanup crews is now called bioremediation, and it is big business. More than fifty bioremediation companies use microbes to clean the soil at former industrial plants, military ammunitions sites, and old gasoline stations.

Gasoline is the most common contaminant of groundwater throughout the United States. Thousands of steel tanks buried beneath old gas stations are corroding and leaking gas into the soil. "These tanks are everywhere; it's a nationwide problem,"[24] says Loring Nies, an assistant professor of environmental engineering at Purdue University. Before microbes were used, the soil had to be completely removed down to depths of several feet—an expensive and labor-intensive process.

Rusty barrels containing toxic materials can release toxins into the soil. Using microbes to clean up such waste has become a common practice.

Now microbes that occur naturally in the soil are "fed" by pumping phosphorus and nitrogen into the ground, promoting rapid bacterial growth.

Another type of bacteria that likes to eat poison is cleaning up old contaminated mining sites. Gold is traditionally separated from ore using cyanide, a highly toxic substance that can kill within minutes if ingested. After processing, the cyanide is washed away and ends up in nearby streams and creeks. The Homestake Mine in South Dakota, the largest gold mine in North America, had been washing cyanide into Whitewood Creek for more than a hundred years. The creek was so polluted that it was thought to be sterile: Nothing could live in it. But when researchers tested the creek water, they found that one type of bacteria was thriving. That bacterium used the poisonous cyanide as its main food source. Now that bacterium is being used to clean up other mining sites as well.

Researchers around the world search for bacteria with useful appetites. Some, like the mining microbes, are found in nature, while others are discovered in an endless array of laboratory tests. At the University of West Florida scientists tested more than twenty thousand mutant strains of bacteria before they found one that turned a toxic industrial chemical, TCE (trichloroethylene), into a harmless substance. Today bacteria are used to detoxify soil and water polluted by PCBs (polychlorinated biphenyls), creosote, DDT, and other tough, toxic compounds.

The USGS estimates that cleaning up existing environmental contamination in the country would cost as much as $1 trillion. With bioremediation the cost may be cut drastically and the cleanup will be less stressful on the environment. But much of what bioremediation promises has yet to be realized. Designer microbes will eventually take the place of naturally occurring ones and will be able to do the job faster and more efficiently. One recent project at the Oak Ridge

National Laboratory in Tennessee involved adding a bioluminescent gene to one toxin eater to make it glow so that human cleanup crews could see the bacteria at work.

Even *The Guinness Book of World Records* "World's Toughest Bacterium"[25] is being put to work. *Deincoccus radiodurans* was discovered in 1956 inside a can of meat that had spoiled despite being sterilized by radiation. This amazing bacterium can withstand and actually grow during exposure to 3 million rads of radiation, which is more than one thousand times the amount of radiation needed to kill a human. The bacterium does become damaged during exposure, but in less than one day, it is able to repair its damaged chromosomes. Scientists working with the Department of Energy are looking into the possibility of using these microbes, or hybrids of them, to clean up radioactive sites left over from the production of nuclear weapons.

Microbes and Masterpieces

Perhaps the most astounding use of microbes can be found in the back rooms of major art institutions where the microbes' voracious appetites are being let loose on priceless masterpieces, such as the *Conversion and Battle of Saint Efisio* by Spinello Aretino. Many Italian works of art dating back to the fourteenth century were severely damaged during World War II. Attempts to repair them with glue and harmful cleaning solvents caused even more damage, and after sixty years they were thought to be hopelessly unrepairable.

But in 2003, researchers used microbes for the first time to remove the damaging glue. The bacterium *Pseudomonas stutzeri* was applied to the canvases using damp wool compresses. The bacterium quickly ate the harmful residue, almost magically revealing the original pigments underneath. Within twelve hours,

A researcher uses microbes to restore an Italian masterpiece to its original magnificence.

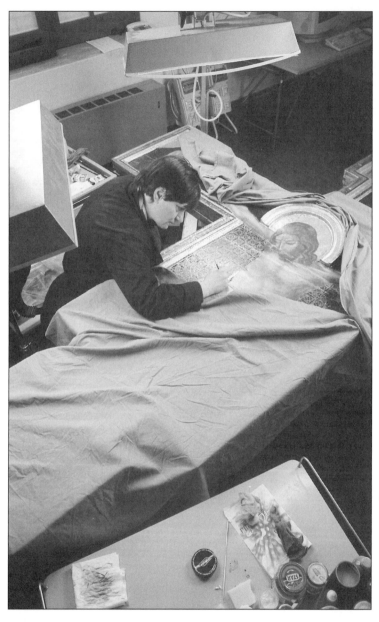

80 percent of the paintings were clean, and the figures were recognizable for the first time in many years.

Much of what microbes have been used for is cleaning up our mistakes: damaged works of art, environmental oil spills, and toxic pollution. But what does the future hold for man and microbe?

Chapter 6

The Future Under a Microscope

A bacterium was the birthplace of genetic engineering, one of the most revolutionary technologies in science. And since those first experiments with bacteria back in the 1960s, hundreds of new medicines and products have become commonplace. But genetic engineering is only the tip of the microbial iceberg. To understand how microbes work in the world around us and how they affect our lives, scientists are recording their entire genetic code.

Writing the Book of Bacteria

In 1994 the U.S. Department of Energy (DOE) announced the beginning of the Microbial Genome Project. A genome is the complete set of instructions for making any organism. It is the "parts list" of the organism's DNA—the list of letters that represent the base pairs that make up the DNA strand. A single microbial genome may contain between 500,000 to 8 million DNA base pairs; the human genome contains 3 billion. Whereas the Human Genome Project took years to write the "first draft" of the entire genetic material inside a person's cells, most microbes can be sequenced in a matter of weeks or even days. By the end of 2003, more than one hundred bacteria and viruses had been sequenced.

But why would the DOE want to know every letter in the long DNA sequence of a microbe? Scientists want to know because these letters hold the code for the creation of certain proteins that carry out various functions within the cell. Some genes instruct the production of certain proteins to make the cell wall, while others instruct the cell to manufacture hydrogen or to infect liver tissue. But just as a parts list of a car's engine does not explain the assembly and function of the car, the genome does not provide information about what the parts do. Another project called Genome for Life, an extension of the Microbial Genome Project, is seeking to understand the function of the genes that have been written down.

According to Daniel W. Drell of the DOE and his colleagues, "We can now look at how the 'parts' come together in ways that challenge basic science and offer concrete applications in a range of issues affecting, for example, water quality, environmental remediation, and medicine." [26] The hope is that microbes will prove to be a source of new genes that can be used to solve problems that confront society today. The DOE is most interested in microbes that can address environmental problems, such as global warming and toxic waste cleanup, or lead to new sources of clean, environmentally friendly energy.

Global Warming

Over the past decades scientists have found that Earth's temperature is rising more rapidly than expected, and they predict another rise of 1.5 to 4.5 degrees centigrade over the next one hundred years. This rise in temperature is due to the increased amount of carbon dioxide (CO_2) and other greenhouse gases that are released into the atmosphere from industrial processes. They eat away at the ozone layer, which protects the earth from the sun's harmful rays. Coupled with changing land use and deforestation, these gases have long-term effects on the planet. Increased temperatures can lead to a rise in the ocean's water levels, which erodes coastlines. It could trigger floods and drastically change ecosystems.

But what if there were microbes that ate excess CO_2? In 1991 two Japanese microbiologists who were exploring ways to maintain the atmosphere discovered a bacterium called *Synechococcus*, which thrives on CO_2. The scientists believe that knowing the genome of CO_2-consuming bacteria could lead to the future development of huge bioreactors filled with bacteria feeding off of unwanted CO_2 in the atmosphere.

Scientists hope to use microbes to eliminate excess carbon dioxide in the atmosphere and reverse the effects of global warming in the Arctic and other areas.

Extreme Genes

Many of the microbes that the DOE researchers have selected for the genome project live in extreme places. "The diversity and range of their environmental adaptations indicate that microbes long ago 'solved' many problems for which scientists are still actively seeking solutions."[27]

For example, the bacterium *Methanococcus jannaschii* grows in thermal vents eight thousand feet below the ocean off the coast of Baja California. It thrives under high pressure and temperatures as hot as 190 degrees Fahrenheit. It exists in anaerobic conditions and produces methane gas. *M. jannaschii* is being studied as a working model for the production of methane as a useful, renewable energy source.

When scientists know the code for what makes a bacterium operate, they will also know how to control it. And comparing the genomes of one bacterium to another will allow scientists to see patterns of function and predict what other microbes are capable of doing.

So far the genome researchers have been awed by the amount of previously unidentified genes they have uncovered from some of these extreme microbes. More than half of the genes sequenced in *M. jannaschii,* for example, were completely unknown to science. This means that the proteins that the genes instruct the cell to create are also unknown. They offer an amazing new resource to explore. The genome project is bringing to light a vast menu of genetic ingredients of genes and proteins that can be used to genetically engineer new microbes and new products.

The DOE is not the only place that is sequencing the genes of microbes. Medical institutions focus on the bacteria and viruses that cause disease. If scientists can figure out which genes are responsible for the cause and means of infection, then they can target those genes with drug therapy.

A Vaccine for Cancer

Most people think of a virus as something that should be avoided, but for years we have used weakened forms of viruses to combat smallpox, polio, chicken pox, measles, and mumps. Now researchers are hoping to add cancer to that list.

Emptied of its contents, a virus's capsid becomes a durable container capable of withstanding all sorts of toxic environments and able to transport many different chemicals and drugs to a specific location. Viral containers are already being used to deliver magnetic material to tumor cells so that they can be seen in magnetic resonance imaging (MRI) tests, and they are now being tested for use in delivering cancer cures.

The part of a virus that makes it a perfect medical tool is its ability to target a specific type of cell. The drugs currently used to treat cancer circulate throughout the entire body. They act on healthy cells as well as cancerous cells, causing many side effects that can be quite severe. But viruses are very specific. They target only the cells they are programmed to infect and leave other cells alone. Scientists around the world are looking at ways to use the virus's natural targeting characteristic to zero in on specific cancerous tumor cells.

At the Institute for Cancer Studies at Birmingham University in England, researchers are working on an experimental therapy using a genetically modified virus as a homing device for cancer-killing drugs. It is called VDEPT, short for virus-directed enzyme prodrug therapy.

Researchers are studying the use of genetically altered viruses to target and eliminate cancerous cells like these lung cancer cells.

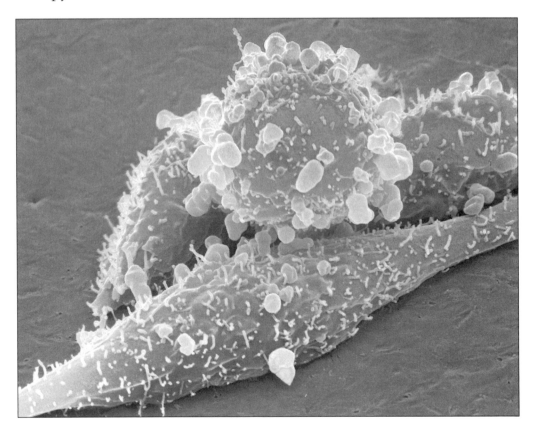

A patient would first be injected with the specially designed virus that infects only cancer cells. Then an injection of the prodrug is given. The prodrug is a chemical that is harmless to healthy cells, but when it comes in contact with the virus-infected cancer cell, it becomes deadly. The cancer cells take it in, and the drug is transformed into a toxic substance that kills the tumor cell instantly. Healthy cells remain unaffected.

Virus Vectors

Scientists are experimenting with viruses not only to distribute a needed vaccine but also to deliver healthy

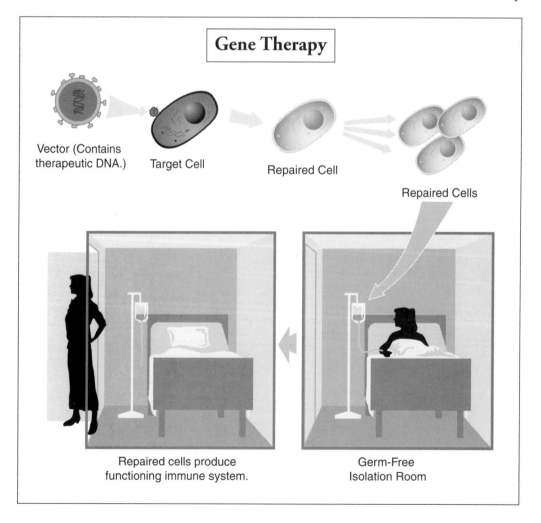

Gene Therapy

Vector (Contains therapeutic DNA.)

Target Cell

Repaired Cell

Repaired Cells

Repaired cells produce functioning immune system.

Germ-Free Isolation Room

genes to cells with a genetic disorder, a procedure called gene therapy. Gene therapy could help patients who have a genetic disorder like cystic fibrosis or sickle-cell anemia, where only one or two missing or defective genes are involved.

In gene therapy RNA retroviruses are first rendered harmless. Then the healthy genes are inserted into the virus's genome. The altered virus is then injected into the tissue where it actively seeks out the appropriate cells to infect. As the RNA is copied by the cell's reproductive machinery, it is also incorporated into the cell's DNA.

This procedure is still in an experimental stage, but one of the first patients to benefit was an eighteen-month-old boy in England. He had a rare genetic disorder called severe combined immunodeficiency that prevented him from developing an immune system. He lived his first eighteen months in a plastic, sterile bubble room. Doctors removed bone marrow from the boy and used a virus to carry a new working version of the missing gene into immune cells in the marrow. The marrow was put back into the boy's leg, where it gradually started to produce healthy white cells that now protect the boy from infection.

One problem doctors must overcome is the unpredictability of where the new gene is inserted in the patient's DNA strand. If the placement is not exact, then the gene will not express itself. Scientists also have to battle with the patient's immune system, which seeks out and destroys these virus vectors before they get a chance to deliver their genetic package.

Even though gene therapy is still in the experimental stage, it has caused much controversy. Many people are concerned about the safety of the procedure as well as the long-term effects of inserting a virus, even a disabled one, into a person's body.

Nanotechnology

Viruses are making their mark in industry too, where they are being used as spare parts and miniature tools

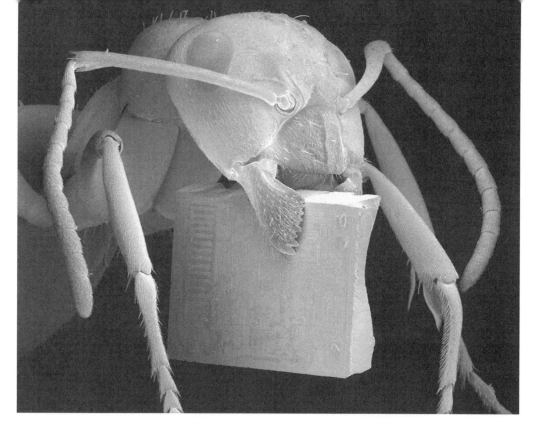

An electron micrograph shows an ant holding a tiny microchip. Viruses can potentially be used to create even smaller, more efficient microchips.

in the growing field of nanotechnology. *Nanotechnology* is the term given to research and engineering done at an atomic or molecular level. *Nano* means one-billionth, and a nanometer is one-billionth of a meter.

Small is big in science. When Nobel Prize–winning physicist Richard Feynman declared in 1960, "There's plenty of room at the bottom," [28] he meant that technology can always get smaller. In 1946, when the first computer was constructed, it filled two thousand square feet of space and weighed fifty tons. Today the smallest microcomputer would fit on the head of a matchstick, and the smallest microchip, unveiled in 2003 by a Malaysian company, is no bigger than the period at the end of this sentence. But the smaller technology gets, the more necessary it becomes to study those organisms that perform complex tasks on that level every day—microbes.

"Scientists didn't invent nanoscience," says Angela Belcher, a pioneering materials chemist at Massachusetts Institute of Technology. "Organisms have been doing if for a long time." [29]

Belcher started out studying how sea snails made their beautiful mother-of-pearl shells. The snail stacks individual molecules of calcium carbonate into layers to form a beautifully luminescent and very strong shell. Belcher uses the same technique of building a new material molecule by molecule, but she gets viruses to do the hard work for her.

Viruses make a good workforce because they have evolved over millions of years to work perfectly at the nanoscale level. It is also easy to alter a virus's genetic material and instruct it to perform a specific task. The viruses that Belcher and most nanoscientists use are bacteriophages because they infect only bacteria. These viruses are genetically modified to grow certain protein receptors on their surface so that they are able to bind like a magnet to specific particles. This process takes about three weeks.

One such virus strain is able to bind to zinc sulphide, a semiconductor, which means it can transmit an electrical current. Billions of these specially made viruses bind to billions of zinc particles. In a solution, viruses normally organize themselves in almost military precision so that they move freely without bumping into one another or creating a logjam. As these viruses with their zinc particles self-organize, they form an extremely thin film that can be picked up out of the solution with a pair of tweezers. This thin film acts like the liquid crystal display on computer monitors. Belcher believes that her viruses can create stronger, smaller, and potentially more complex materials than those produced by man-made machines. The process is also clean; it does not pollute the environment.

In another lab researchers are working to perfect viral wire. The bacteriophage viruses are altered to bind to other particles, but only at the ends of their long, skinny bodies. They latch on to each other, end to end, like children's snap-together beads, forming long chains of microscopic semiconducting wire.

Silver-Making Bacteria

Creating any kind of material on a nanoscale is costly and complex, but if bacteria can collect particles of a precious metal like silver, it could be invaluable. In a Swedish laboratory, scientists are working with an unusual strain of bacteria that does just that. They crank out tiny crystals of silver.

Silver is usually toxic to most microbes and is used in several bacteria-killing substances, but *Pseudomonas stutzeri* seems to thrive on it. This bacterium, which is the same microbe that is used to clean paintings, was found growing on rocks in a silver mine. The bacterium gathers up the metal and bundles it in distinct crystal shapes at the edge of its cell. These microscopic silver particles can then be harvested to construct extremely thin, light-sensitive metal film or coatings for solar collectors, or tiny optical and electronic devices.

Bacterial Batteries

How could a tiny electronic device made out of microscopic particles of silver be powered? Some researchers are taking their cue from the science fiction *Matrix* movies, in which humans are used as living batteries, and learning how to harness a living electrical source. Fortunately they are not using humans, as the movies portray; instead, they are creating microbial fuel cells and bacterial batteries.

Like any living organism, bacteria take in and expel energy. A colony of *E. coli* bacteria takes in carbohydrates, such as sugar, and breaks them down with enzymes. The bacteria release energy in the form of hydrogen, the same substance that fuels "green" cars. The electrical current comes in the form of a steady flow of electrons released as the microbe eats.

One company in England has made a fuel cell that is the size of a personal CD player. The bacteria inside feed on sugar cubes. Chemical reactions strip electrons from the hydrogen atoms to produce a voltage that can power an electrical circuit. To make it more cost-effective, researchers are developing a second model that would be fueled by organic waste material, such as the leftovers from lunch. Currently, the microbial fuel cell is being used to power a small robot around the lab.

The U.S. Department of Defense is interested in another microbial fuel cell that uses a bacteria found on the bottom of the sea floor. *Rhodoferax ferrireducens* can convert more than 80 percent of the sugar it eats to electricity. The process is slow. One cup of sugar can light up a 60-watt bulb for seventeen hours, but the process to do so takes a week to charge up. The advantage to this slow process is that once it gets going, the battery continues to work without interruption—a good quality to have in a battery that is difficult to access. The Department of Defense is eyeballing microbial fuel cells to power electronic monitoring devices located at the

The electrical current released as a microbe eats can be harnessed to create efficient fuel cells like this one.

bottom of the ocean. These fuel cells would run off of the organic sediment found on the sea floor.

Other fuel cells are being adapted to power medical ventilators and generate electricity for pacemakers. The pacemaker battery would run off of glucose, the sugar found in the pacemaker-wearer's blood.

Microbial Motors

Imagine a microscopic device propelled by a nanoscale motor that could buzz through the body in search of specific cells. That is the target goal for engineers at Cornell University. Researchers combined a molecule made by a bacterium with one made by a scientist in the lab. The result was a motor that operates similarly to an *E. coli* bacterium turning its flagella on and off.

The *E. coli* uses the enzyme ATP to send signals to its flagella so that it can move around. Instead of flagella, researchers attached an engineered nanoscale rotor to act as the motor's moving part. The rotor rotates in response to electrochemical reactions with charged parts of the ATP molecule. This specially designed *E. coli* bacterium could be tethered to a fixed spot and used as a tiny pump in industrial and medical devices.

The Future

Powering pacemakers with a bacterial battery, curing cancer with a virus, or cooking over a gas stove fueled by methane-producing microbes from the backyard septic tank may seem far-fetched, but they could become common events in the future.

Each year we become more aware of the influence of the mighty microbe. Looking into the past, we see that microbes have had the power to change human history. Experiencing the infectious diseases of today, we know that microbes can end a person's life, diminish a village's population, and devastate a country's economy. But they can also be the solution to many of our problems in the future.

Whatever our technology needs may be or whatever problems confront us—from emerging disease to en-

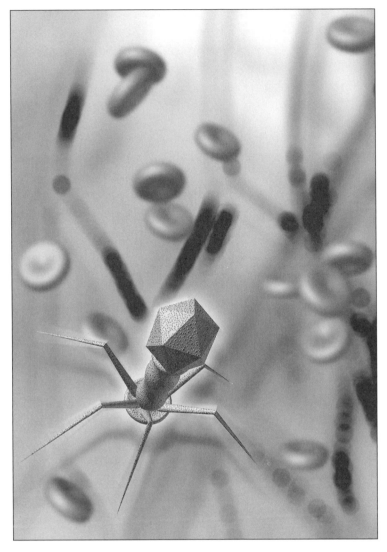

Although microbes like this virus have caused illness and death throughout history, the ability to harness their power for human benefit holds considerable promise for the future.

vironmental damage—there will be a microbe some-where that is able to help, but only if people are wise enough to discover it. Such discoveries will take time. Scientists have only been aware of bacteria and their effect on humans for less than three hundred years. And they have only scratched the surface of the world of viruses. Their understanding of these microorgan-isms and their power continues to grow, along with an appreciation of what man and microbe can do together. Researchers can learn how to maintain the atmosphere from studying bacteria that have been doing just that for millions of years, and medical doctors can discover how to keep people healthy by examining the viruses that infect them.

The key to harnessing bacteria and viruses for good is to appreciate the possible consequences of the bad, because our relationship with the microbial world is a two-way street. Humans' behavior affects microbial behavior, and vice versa. We might not see the next devastating infectious bacteria or virus barreling down on us, but with the use of other microbes, we will have the tools and knowledge to combat it. It is simple. Bacteria and viruses are our worst enemies, yet they are also vital for our survival. We live in a sea of invisible microbes, and we can either sink or swim.

Notes

Chapter 1: We Are Surrounded

1. Quoted in Robert S. Boyd, "Despite Bad Reputation, Bacteria Are Vital to Life," *Buffalo News,* June 22, 2003, p. H-6.
2. Quoted in Boyd, "Despite Bad Reputation," p. H-6.
3. J. William Schopf, *Cradle of Life: The Discovery of Earth's Earliest Fossils.* Princeton, NJ: Princeton University Press, 1999, p. 3.
4. Quoted in Arno Karlen, *Man and Microbes: Disease and Plagues in History and Modern Times.* New York: Putnam's, 1995, p. 55.
5. Quoted in Kathy A. Svitil, "Did Viruses Make Us Human?" *Discover,* November 2002. www.discover.com.

Chapter 2: Early Discoveries

6. Quoted in William M. Bowsky, *The Black Death: A Turning Point in History?* New York: Holt, Rinehart & Winston, 1971, p. 13.
7. Quoted in Bowsky, *The Black Death,* p. 13.
8. Quoted in James Cross Giblin, *When Plague Strikes: The Black Death, Smallpox, AIDS.* New York: HarperCollins, 1995, p. 70.
9. Quoted in Giblin, *When Plague Strikes,* p. 76.
10. Quoted in Giblin, *When Plague Strikes,* p. 32.
11. Quoted in History Learning Site, "Medicine in Ancient Rome," 2002. www.historylearningsite.co.uk.
12. Quoted in Warnar Moll, "Antonie van Leeuwenhoek Delft Biography," 2003. www.eronet.nl/users/warnar/leeuwenhoek.html.
13. Quoted in Moll, "Antonie van Leeuwenhoek."
14. Quoted in David M. Locke, *Viruses: The Smallest Enemy.* New York: Crown, 1974, p. 20.

Chapter 3: Fighting an Invisible Enemy

15. Quoted in Giblin, *When Plague Strikes,* p. 95.
16. Quoted in Jenner Museum, "The Final Conquest of the Speckled Monster," 2003. www.jennermuseum.com.

17. Quoted in Pete Moore, *Killer Germs: Rogue Diseases of the Twenty-first Century.* London: Carlton, 2001, p. 7.
18. Quoted in Giblin, *When Plague Strikes,* p. 143.
19. Quoted in Michael Shnayerson and Mark J. Plotkin, *The Killers Within: The Deadly Rise of Drug-Resistant Bacteria.* Boston: Little, Brown, 2002, p. 35.

Chapter 4: Emerging Microbes
20. Quoted in Boyd, "Despite Bad Reputation," p. H-6.
21. Quoted in Boyd, "Despite Bad Reputation," p. H-6.
22. Quoted in Nancy Shute, "SARS Hits Home," *U.S. News & World Report,* May 5, 2003, p. 40.
23. Quoted in Stephen S. Hall, "On the Trail of the West Nile Virus," *Smithsonian,* July 2003, p. 94.

Chapter 5: Harnessing Invisible Power
24. Quoted in *Purdue News,* "Munching Microbes Make a Meal out of Toxic Substances," April 1997. www.purdue.edu.
25. *The Guinness Book of World Records.* Stamford, CT: Guinness Media, 1998, p. 316.

Chapter 6: The Future Under a Microscope
26. Daniel W. Drell, Anna Palmisano, and Marvin E. Frazier, "Microbial Genomes: An Information Base for 21st Century Microbiology," U.S. Department of Energy, 2000. www.sc.doe.gov.
27. U.S. Department of Energy, Office of Science, Office of Biological and Environmental Research, "Microbial Genomics Research," 2003, p. 1.
28. Richard P. Feynman, "There's Plenty of Room at the Bottom," *Engineering & Science,* February 1960, p. 1.
29. Quoted in Deborah Smith, "Starting Small: Scientist Uses Viruses as Building Blocks for New Technology," SMH.com.au, 2003. www.smh.com.au.

Glossary

anaerobic: Without oxygen.

antibiotic: A substance that kills a bacterial infection.

bacteria: Microscopic one-celled organisms (bacterium: a single organism).

bacteriophage: A virus that infects bacteria.

bioremediation: The process of cleaning up the environment using microbes.

capsid: The protein coat of a virus.

cyanobacteria: A type of bacteria once called blue-green algae.

DNA (deoxyribonucleic acid): The genetic material, found in the nucleus of a living cell, that carries the information about an organism and contains the codes needed to build proteins.

enzyme: A protein that controls chemical reactions.

flagella: Long, whiplike tails on some types of bacteria that allow them to move.

genetic engineering: The alteration of genetic material in an organism; involves the transfer of DNA from one cell to another.

genome: The complete sequence of DNA base pairs that code for a specific organism.

lymphocyte: A type of white blood cell that produces antibodies.

microbe: A microscopic organism.

microbiology: The scientific study of microscopic organisms.

nanometer: An extremely small unit of measure; one-billionth of a meter.

nanotechnology: Research and engineering performed at a molecular level.

pathogen: A disease-causing organism.

phagocyte: A type of white blood cell that engulfs and destroys harmful bacteria.

plasmid: A small, circular molecule of DNA found in bacteria.

spore: A single bacterial cell covered with a special protective coat that allows it to remain in a resting state.

vaccine: A substance made from dead or weakened bacteria or viruses used to inoculate a person in order to prevent a disease and produce an immunity to it.

vector: An animal or insect that carries a bacteria or virus but is not harmed by it.

virus: A disease-producing particle composed of genetic material covered with a protein coat; a virus only can reproduce in a living cell.

For Further Reading

Books

Howard and Margery Facklam, *Bacteria*. New York: Twenty-first Century, 1994. A fascinating and easy-to-read description of bacteria, their place in the world, and their effect on our lives.

————, *Viruses*. New York: Twenty-first Century, 1994. A concise introduction to the world of viruses and the scientists who discovered them.

Mark Friedlander, *Outbreak: Disease Detectives at Work*. Minneapolis: Lerner, 2000. Recounts the work performed by epidemiologists from the Centers for Disease Control during infectious disease outbreaks.

James Cross Giblin, *When Plague Strikes: The Black Death, Smallpox, AIDS*. New York: HarperCollins, 1995. Fascinating accounts of three major diseases and how they changed the world.

Cynthia S. Gross, *The New Biotechnology: Putting Microbes to Work*. Minneapolis: Lerner, 1988. A good introduction to genetic engineering and the use of bacteria in industry.

Lisa Yount, *Epidemics*. San Diego: Lucent, 2000. Discusses the return of epidemics in modern times, the possible causes, and how they are tracked and controlled.

Web Sites

Centers for Disease Control and Prevention (www.cdc.gov). Contains up-to-date information on emerging diseases and the CDC's responses to them.

Digital Learning Center for Microbial Ecology (http://commtech lab.msu.edu). Very kid friendly; includes the Microbial Zoo, Microbe of the Month, and Microbes in the News.

The Jenner Museum (www.jennermuseum.com). Provides an introduction to Edward Jenner, his life, and his work eradicating smallpox.

Microbe World (www.microbe.org). Run by the American Society for Microbiology; includes fun experiments as well as information about careers in microbiology.

Microbial Genomics Gateway (www.microbialgenome.org). Gives background information about microbes, their importance in the world, and the Microbial Genome Project.

World Health Organization (www.who.int/en). Provides current information on a variety of health issues that threaten people around the world.

Works Consulted

Books

Nicholas Bakalar, *Where the Germs Are: A Scientific Safari*. New York: Wiley, 2003. A vivid description of microbes encountered in everyday life.

Wayne Biddle, *A Field Guide to Germs*. New York: Holt, 1995. Short excerpts that describe the natural history of the microbes that cause disease.

William M. Bowsky, *The Black Death: A Turning Point in History?* New York: Holt, Rinehart & Winston, 1971. Discusses the effect that the bubonic plague had on human civilization.

Bill Bryson, *A Short History of Nearly Everything*. New York: Broadway, 2003. An entertaining compilation that includes one chapter on the power of microbes.

Paul De Kruif, *Microbe Hunters*. New York: Harcourt, Brace, 1953. A collection of short biographies of famous and not-so-famous microbiologists.

Bernard Dixon, *Magnificent Microbes: An Astonishing Look Inside the Microscopic World of Man's Invisible Allies*. New York: Atheneum, 1976. A classic edition in microbiology that is written in layman's terms by a trained microbiologist.

———, *Power Unseen: How Microbes Rule the World*. Oxford: Freeman, 1994. A portrait gallery of seventy-five microbes and their characteristic behaviors.

David B. Dusenbery, *Life at Small Scale: The Behavior of Microbes*. New York: Scientific American Library, 1996. A comprehensive and technical book on bacteria and viruses.

The Guinness Book of World Records. Stamford, CT: Guiness Media, 1998. This book contains records such as "World's Largest Virus" that are interesting and sometimes obscure.

Brent Hoff and Carter Smith, *Mapping Epidemics: A Historical Atlas of Disease*. New York: Franklin Watts, 2000. A fact-filled atlas of diseases throughout history.

Arno Karlen, *Man and Microbes: Disease and Plagues in History and Modern Times*. New York: Putnam's, 1995. Recounts man's and microbes' history from the first recorded encounter to the present day.

David M. Locke, *Viruses: The Smallest Enemy*. New York: Crown, 1974. This is an older book, but it effectively highlights the early discoveries in viral research.

Pete Moore, *Killer Germs: Rogue Diseases of the Twenty-first Century*. London: Carlton, 2001. An eye-opening account of antibiotic-resistant bacteria, emergent diseases, and bioterrorism.

Cynthia Needham, Mahlon Hoagland, Kenneth McPherson, and Bert Dodson, *Intimate Strangers: Unseen Life on Earth*. Washington, DC: ASM, 2000. A printed version of a National Science Foundation television documentary of microbes' role on Earth.

J. William Schopf, *Cradle of Life: The Discovery of Earth's Earliest Fossils*. Princeton, NJ: Princeton University Press, 1999. An account of the discovery of the earliest fossils of bacteria found in Australia.

Michael Shnayerson and Mark J. Plotkin, *The Killers Within: The Deadly Rise of Drug-Resistant Bacteria*. Boston: Little, Brown, 2002. A narrative account of doctors and research scientists who encounter and battle drug-resistant bacteria.

Jack Uldrich and Deb Newberry, *The Next Big Thing Is Really Small*. New York: Crown Business, 2002. An introduction to nanotechnology and its impact on industry.

Periodicals

Michael Barletta, "Keeping Track of Anthrax," *Bulletin of the Atomic Scientists,* May/June 2002.

Robert S. Boyd, "Despite Bad Reputation, Bacteria Are Vital to Life," *Buffalo News,* June 22, 2003.

David Brown, "Stopping a Scourge," *Smithsonian,* September 2003.

Richard P. Feynman, "There's Plenty of Room at the Bottom," *Engineering & Science,* February 1960.

Jessica Gorman, "Microbial Materials," *Science News,* July 5, 2003.

Stephen S. Hall, "On the Trail of the West Nile Virus," *Smithsonian,* July 2003.

Claudia Kalb, "The Mystery of SARS," *Newsweek,* May 5, 2003.

Michael Lemonick and Alice Park, "The Truth About SARS," *Time,* May 5, 2003.

Anita Manning, "USA's Disease Detectives Track Epidemics Worldwide," *USA Today,* July 25, 2001.

Marilynn Marchione, "Exotic Diseases Hit Home," *Buffalo News,* June 22, 2003.

Nancy Shute, "SARS Hits Home," *U.S. News & World Report,* May 5, 2003.

Rebecca Skloot, "Angela Belcher," *Popular Science,* November 2002.

John Travis, "Gut Check: The Bacteria in Your Intestines Are Welcome Guests," *Science News,* May 31, 2003.

U.S. Department of Energy, Office of Science, Office of Biological and Environmental Research, "Microbial Genomics Research," 2003.

Internet Sources

Terry Devitt, "Study of Microbes May Hone Predictions of Mining Impact," *News @ UW-Madison,* 2000. www.news.wisc.edu.

Daniel W. Drell, Anna Palmisano, and Marvin E. Frazier, "Microbial Genomes: An Information Base for 21st Century Microbiology," U.S. Department of Energy, 2000. www.sc.doe.gov.

History Learning Site, "Medicine in Ancient Rome," 2002. www.historylearningsite.co.uk.

Mark Horstman, "Bizarre Giant Virus Rewrites the Record Books," *News in Science,* March 31, 2003. www.abc.net.au.

Jennifer F. Hughes and John M. Coffin, "The Origin and the Sickening of Our Species," *Popular Science,* December 2001. www.popsci.com.

Jenner Museum, "The Final Conquest of the Speckled Monster," 2003. www.jennermuseum.com.

Rossella Lorenzi, "Bacteria Restores Ancient Italian Frescoes," *Discovery News.com,* June 20, 2003. http://dsc.discovery.com.

Warnar Moll, "Antonie van Leeuwenhoek Delft Biography," 2003. www.eronet.nl.

Purdue News, "Munching Microbes Make a Meal out of Toxic Substances," April 1997. www.purdue.edu.

Rosalind Schrempf, "World's Toughest Bacterium Has a Taste for Waste," http://pnl.gov.

Seattle Times, "Therapy Uses Viruses as Natural Antibiotics," June 17, 2003. http://seattletimes.nwsource.com.

Deborah Smith, "Starting Small: Scientist Uses Viruses as Building Blocks for New Technology," SMH.com.au, 2003. www.smh.com.au.

Kathy A. Svitil, "Did Viruses Make Us Human?" *Discover,* November 2002. www.discover.com.

U.S. Geological Survey, "Bioremediation: Nature's Way to a Cleaner Environment," 2002. http://water.usgs.gov.

Index

105

Picture Credits

About the Author

Peggy Thomas is the author of ten nonfiction books for children and young adults as well as numerous magazine and newspaper articles. Several of her books have been placed on the New York Public Library's recommended list of Books for the Teen Age and listed as an NSTA-CBC Outstanding Science Trade Book for Children. Thomas received her master's degree in anthropology from the State University of New York at Buffalo and lives in Middleport, New York, with her husband and two children.